THE ART OF TREASURE ISLAND

PORTALS OF THE PACIFIC

THE ART OF
TREASURE ISLAND

BY EUGEN NEUHAUS

*First-hand Impressions of the Architecture,
Sculpture, Landscape Design, Color Effects,
Mural Decorations, Illumination, and
Other Artistic Aspects of the
Golden Gate International
Exposition of 1939*

UNIVERSITY OF CALIFORNIA PRESS
BERKELEY, CALIFORNIA · 1939

UNIVERSITY OF CALIFORNIA PRESS
BERKELEY, CALIFORNIA

———————

CAMBRIDGE UNIVERSITY PRESS
LONDON, ENGLAND

PRINTED IN THE UNITED STATES OF AMERICA
BY SAMUEL T. FARQUHAR, UNIVERSITY PRINTER

To ARTHUR BROWN, JR., *Architect*

CHAIRMAN OF THE ARCHITECTURAL COMMISSION OF
THE GOLDEN GATE INTERNATIONAL EXPOSITION &
SCHOLARLY EXPONENT OF THE FUNDAMENTALS
OF A NOBLE ART

Moulin photo; courtesy of the California Toll Bridge Authority

SAN FRANCISCO-OAKLAND BAY BRIDGE FROM YERBA BUENA ISLAND

Contents

ix

Illustrations

TREASURE ISLAND FROM YERBA BUENA ISLAND

xvi

THE MARINA AND YERBA BUENA ISLAND

Chapter I

THE SIGNIFICANCE OF EXPOSITIONS

ROMANTIC and epochal events such as the Golden Gate International Exposition are justly regarded as milestones of human progress. They so vividly and indelibly impress themselves upon our minds that, in retrospect, they help us to recall major happenings in our lives. And they provide the historian with important data on the progress of nations and of the world at large.

International expositions of the size and scope of the present one are of relatively recent origin, although fairs of all kinds antedate them by centuries; indeed, as early as 1268 the first fair of the Christian era was held, at Venice. It consisted of a grand display, a water fête on the Grand Canal, and a procession of the trades. The various guilds of Venice marched through the narrow streets to the great square of St. Mark's and there asked the dogaressa—the wife of the reigning doge—to inspect the products of their industry. Since then, many fairs have been held in Europe and, in the more recent years, in America. All the important continental cities, from Stockholm to Rome and from Madrid to Nizhnii Novgorod, have had their trade fairs—fairs limited to a display of the products of the country or city in which they were held—and some of these have become annual events, as for instance the sample fair at Leipzig, which still flourishes. These mercantile fairs, being known all over the civilized world and attended by merchants from every land, were in a sense international; but it was not until the middle of the last century—to be exact, in 1851—that the first truly international exposition came into being. It was international not only because it was visited by representatives of many nationalities, but also because, for the first time, foreign nations were represented by buildings contributed and maintained at their expense. This first truly international exposition was held at London, and was so great a success that other nations soon sought to imitate it.

At the International Exposition of 1855, at Paris, there was first presented a feature of great cultural interest which was to be an important one in almost all later world's fairs—an exhibit of the fine arts. At the first international exposition in the United States, held at Philadelphia in 1876, there was introduced another idea, the commemoration of a historical event; and it is as the centennial celebration of the declaration of our national independence that the Philadelphia exposition is today proudly remembered in the history of the United States. Several other expositions held in this country have been occasions of celebrating in retrospect some historical event—the discovery of America (Chicago, 1893), the Louisiana Purchase (St. Louis, 1904), the completion of the Panama Canal (San Francisco, 1915). Chicago in 1933 boldly summed up a whole "century of progress," and this year New York, instead of looking backward into the past, looks forward into the future and celebrates a Utopia to be created out of the technical discoveries and the tools of the present age. Our own fair celebrates the completion of two gigantic engineering projects, the Golden Gate bridge and the Bay bridge, technical achievements universally commented upon and admired. The Golden Gate International Exposition is a world on parade, gathered together to rejoice and to give expression to its pride in great works done, and to expand both its practical and its romantic interest in the lands of the Pacific Basin.

An exposition, however, is not merely a festive occasion liberating the spirit and inviting men to forget the routine of ordinary life in an environment that transports them to enchanted isles, distant arcadias, or synthetic utopias. In this country, expositions since the one held at Chicago have also been demonstrations of civic values normally not attainable within the established framework of our cities. Not infrequently, ideas regarded as too imaginative or too impractical have actually been realized—though often in ephemeral form, it is true—within our expositions.

A great fair like the present one employs the talents of a selected group of artists and artisans working, under competent leadership and centralized authority, toward a single purpose. Here architect, sculptor, painter, decorator, and landscape designer enjoy almost ideal opportunities for the free exercise of their talents. Such opportunities as an exposition offers rarely present themselves in the normal life of the artist, and an exposition may well become the supreme test of his creative abilities. True enough, the limitations of time do not always permit sufficiently intensive study of all the possibilities of a given problem; but the unification of the best efforts of many artists and the high degree of imaginative fancy displayed compensate for particulars that may seem too exuberant in ideas or lacking in craftsmanship.

Unfortunately, exposition values in terms of civic art and city planning are not attainable in the haphazard development of cities—at least not in the United States, where the continual shifting of authority with its varying ideals hardly permits, or at least delays, the realization of monumental ideas. In a democracy a comprehensive plan for the artistic development of a city is rarely possible of realization unless it is in the relatively small nucleus we call the civic center or in such of our urban developments as are controlled by a single authority. Any projected monumental civic development that encroaches upon the rights of the individual property owner is likely to be resented if not actually interfered with, and a plan involving the artistic shaping of large areas of a city is at best very slow and in the end too often results in a compromise.

The present exposition, then, like the one held at San Francisco in 1915, is an impressive demonstration of planning on a monumental scale, and it presents a concrete though temporary lesson with a far-reaching significance that every citizen should take to heart. In Europe, with its old and well-ordered cities, expositions are often integrated into existing communities. They are not built on an empty lot away from the center of a city, to be folded up at closing time like an itinerant circus. Almost every exposition in Europe of the last seventy-five years has left a permanent residue in the city in which it was projected.

3

Paris, the exposition city *par excellence* for nearly a century, has always managed to improve permanently some urban area through the agency of its many periodic expositions. In London, Berlin, and Stockholm, and in many other European cities, permanent additions have been recorded in terms of public buildings, recreational and pleasure areas, monumental bridges, squares and open spaces, and civic sculpture. Seville and Barcelona, for example, in 1930 gained many permanent buildings. In America, something of this sort has been achieved occasionally. Chicago in 1893 gained the nucleus for a great recreational area and, what is more important, the impetus for the great plan governing its later remarkable development. St. Louis in 1904 acquired spacious and valuable recreational areas, and a campus for Washington University. San Francisco in 1914, looking forward to the Panama-Pacific International Exposition which was to be opened the next year, obtained, by making a special effort, a permanent auditorium for its civic center. Later it acquired also an artistic legacy in the exposition's Palace of Fine Arts; and indeed much of the subsequent artistic development of the city may be traced to the exposition of 1915. San Diego in 1916 transformed an arid area into a great and permanent park. The Seattle exposition bequeathed to the University of Washington a campus site and valuable buildings.

The main argument often made against all expositions is their great cost for only temporary values. However, if we look upon expositions as laboratories in city planning, we may conclude that although an exposition may perhaps not pay in terms of the auditor's office, its intangible values may eventually compensate for what may at the time have seemed an extravagance.

Unfortunately, the Golden Gate International Exposition has no promise of any permanent tangible civic asset. After it has run its relatively brief course, the site so magically created and transformed will be cleared to become an aviation field of the Federal government. The Administration Building and the two aviation hangars—one of which is temporarily the exposition's art building—will remain as sober reminders of a once inspiring picture. This is hardly enough.

4

THE TOWER OF THE SUN AS SEEN FROM THE COURT OF THE MOON AND STARS

We should make every effort to accomplish some lasting results in applying the inspiring lessons of the Exposition to the permanent improvement of our cities around the Bay and in the West generally. No genuinely patriotic citizen will deny that we have before us one of the major tasks of American life, *"the artistic improvement of our towns and cities to create an environment in which human values may be produced and maintained."*

Since democracies depend upon public consent and approval in any civic improvement, the lessons of an exposition should serve a definite popular educational purpose, especially because the long intervals between expositions rarely offer more than one opportunity of this sort in the lifetime of the citizen unless he is able to travel. World travel, however, is not within the experience of the common man, and the common man in a democracy is, in the last analysis, the important factor in determining the character of his environment.

When the Golden Gate International Exposition was discussed as a project, numerous sites were proposed and investigated. Possibly the motives of the proponents were not entirely disinterested, or each of the proposed sites was for one reason or another found inadequate; at any rate, the upshot was that a site was arbitrarily created, perhaps chiefly to avoid the rivalries of contending political forces. (This, we may recall, was what happened when our Republic had to fix upon a site for a national capital.) No doubt the plastic topography and picturesque landscape of the Bay region offer many attractive localities for the buildings of an exposition. In San Francisco itself, for example, the "panhandle" of Golden Gate Park might conceivably have been extended to the Civic Center and used first as an exposition site and later as a permanent parkway; but obviously the acquisition costs of the property involved, the inevitable litigation, and other practical obstacles would have made such a project impossible within the available time. The decision to place the Exposition on an island yet to be created was not received with much enthusiasm at first, particularly by unimaginative skeptics. But here we have the Exposition as a *fait accompli;* and what does it mean artistically?

7

Rarely has an exposition been created that has had so much to offer in stimulating one's ambitions to re-create, perhaps if only on the smallest scale of a human dwelling, some of its artistic charms. The physical situation of the Exposition is unique in the history of fairs, and appealing to the imagination, and perhaps is not to be recaptured in a permanent way by a single individual. It is frankly an exposition site, absolutely detached from any conflicting, ugly, man-made features such as are much too common in our cities. A magnificent picturesque aggregate of buildings, a veritable *fata morgana,* rises from the waters of San Francisco Bay.

The artistic advantages of this setting are apparent from every direction. To one who on several occasions has had the privilege of traveling abroad, Treasure Island conjures up visions of the island that is dominated by the church of San Giorgio Maggiore opposite the Piazzetta at Venice, with its long, dignified horizontals and the striking vertical accent of a campanile.

Furthermore, not only are the views of Treasure Island entrancing; the many vistas from the island itself are stimulating parts of the whole Exposition scheme. The Exposition everywhere pays its respects to the Bay and its varied borderland. In the west, San Francisco's broken and somewhat jagged outline rises ghostlike, sending its verticals at unexpected places into a mellow sky. To the north and west the Golden Gate bridge in musical, tenuous lines connects the city with the plastic forms of Marin County, surmounted by Mount Tamalpais, the most conspicuous natural landmark in our Bay Region landscape. Alcatraz Island in the foreground, picturesque though it is, looms like an impressive reminder of the sterner aspects of life. To the north, the Bay disappears in suggestive distant forms behind islands and low promontories. Even the hilly landscape around Richmond with its accumulation of industrial structures has a special and artistically not uninteresting character. To the east, Berkeley and Oakland descend to the very edge of the water, presenting a vast panorama of human habitations. On the south, the view from the Exposition is arrested by the wooded slopes of the north side of Yerba Buena Island,

ONE OF THE SOUTH TOWERS

which offer a lush background of live oak and eucalyptus foliage that descends to the edge of a sheltered and placid body of water developed as a harbor and refuge for maritime and pleasure craft.

An island always holds a special fascination, born of mystery and adventure, particularly when it is approachable only by water. True, Treasure Island may be conveniently visited by automobile, and in that way the Bay bridge is added as a thrilling experience. Bay Region residents, by the time the Exposition opened, had accepted the bridges as just another time-saving device, a great convenience. However, a trip over the bridge should always be something of a thrill; physical elevation here results always in an elevation of the spirit.

The plan of the Exposition, which is a result of collaboration among the several architects who constitute its Architectural Commission,* obviously has come out of the formal shape of the island site, a long rectangle with its four corners clipped sharply off. It is a formal plan such as a level area lacking in three-dimensional features suggests. Perhaps an informal shape reflecting the contour of Yerba Buena Island would have been indicated if a great natural park like Golden Gate Park were to be created on Treasure Island; but an aggregate of architectural forms, with its obvious and inescapable commitment to geometric shapes, makes the formal shape obviously more appropriate.

It is regrettable that no effort was made to develop artistically the waterfront of Treasure Island. Nowhere on the island has man an actual close contact with the waters of the Bay. The Bay, unfortunately, is just a barrier, a physical protection against intruders, a substitute for a fence. For climatic and practical reasons the north and west sides could justifiably be ignored in such a scheme, but on the more sheltered east and south sides some architectural features might have taken advantage of the immediate shoreland; there was unquestionably an opportunity to develop outdoor cafés, a belvedere, a boat landing, or at least a promenade over or along the edge of the water.

* The members of the commission, in its initial stage, were Arthur Brown, Jr., W. P. Day, *ex officio* Director of Works, Lewis P. Hobart, William G. Merchant, Timothy L. Pflueger, and Ernest E. Weihe, and the chairman was George Kelham, who deserves a not inconsiderable share of the credit for the design of the plan. After his death in 1937, Arthur Brown, Jr., was appointed chairman.

In the main, the plan of the Exposition is developed upon the use of two main axes, one running almost north and south, the other, shorter and at right angles to it, from east to west. These two major lines intersect at a point emphasized by the central court and the tower of the Exposition. The main buildings on the outside are tied together by plain, relatively low, solid, enclosing, horizontal walls, spaced on either side of these two axes in such a way as to create protected areas of ample size for a succession of garden courts and outdoor recreational and pleasure areas. As it is an established tradition to cast aspersions upon the climate of San Francisco, it will not be amiss to note here that the buildings are designed in such a way as to offer a maximum of shelter from the prevailing summer winds and that they take the fullest advantage of the sun, which during the middle of the day shines into the long north-south axis.

The plan, although formal, is not bisymmetrical like that of the Panama-Pacific Exposition, and is sufficiently varied in its parts to avoid being too obvious or uninteresting. It is essentially monumental and is vaguely recognizable in the grand plan of Paris or Versailles, which is used with many local modifications at Washington, D.C., and indeed anywhere in the world that a monumental impressive decorative effect is desired. It is best appreciated from a great height, as modern aviation has revealed so instructively of many cities in this country and abroad.

The areas outside of this nucleus have been connected with it by wide, tree-lined arteries, which give access to the grounds where stand buildings such as those belonging to the Federal government, the countries of the Pacific area, other foreign countries, California, and other states of the Union.

In contrast to the generally formal plan of the Exposition, the northern extension of its great lagoon has been developed as an informal type of design. The picturesque values which have resulted from this change are a striking succession of delightful vistas created by the union of a naturalistically shaped body of water and man-made elements in terms of exotic buildings surrounded by gardens. Here, unexpected discoveries of intimate and romantic effects may be enjoyed from the seclusion of sheltered coves or from the vantage point of low-arched bridges, bringing back memories of the Palace of Fine Arts of the 1915 exposition.

A very large area at the northern end of the island is given over to those casual devices which are regarded as essential to entertainment and liberating the pent-up emotions. It is appropriately called the Gay-way. Here no preconceived orderly plan has been followed, and the effect is not merely gay, but almost bewildering. Lacking in any kind of recognizable order—which is the requisite of aesthetic pleasure—it does not call for any consideration in this book. The Gayway is the antithesis of the formal Exposition, and its informality, devoid of artistic interest, should serve to emphasize the enduring and enjoyable qualities in the Exposition proper.

Chapter II

THE ARCHITECTURE

IN A DISCUSSION of the "magic city" on Treasure Island, architecture calls for primary consideration. As the visitor approaches the Exposition by automobile and rounds the last curve of the causeway leading down to the gates, the architectural ensemble suddenly reveals itself to him with striking effect. It is undoubtedly from this approach that one receives the most immediate impression of its monumental scale, its variety of styles, its gaiety. The same is true in a lesser degree when the Exposition is approached more gradually by water. Architecture, furthermore, in providing the means for housing the various exhibits, is of great importance for this utilitarian reason alone. Again, architecture is the parent of the arts of sculpture, of painting, and of the various allied decorative arts that are discussed in other chapters of this book.

Although the manifestations of architecture historically rank as the most enduring creations of man, being of stone, steel, brick, and concrete, at Treasure Island we are dealing with a temporary world, a stage-setting for a celebration or a fiesta. We must expect to find here architecture simulating at least outwardly the more permanent stuffs which—particularly in the Old World—have insured to us so many impressive living pictures of the past. These material pretensions of the Exposition should not, however, lessen our enjoyment of the visually effective formal qualities of its architecture. It is with a "willing suspension of disbelief" that we should here approach the ephemeral expression of an otherwise most substantial art.

For this international exposition, particularly as one that was to encompass Occidental and Oriental motifs and ideas, no single style would have been adequate. Many diverse factors had to be pressed into service, and out of this diversity it became necessary to evolve a sense of harmonious unity. The solution of the problem required tact, resourcefulness, ingenuity, and good taste; and it is here that one must congratulate the members of the Architectural Commission for having succeeded conspicuously well. The entirety of the magic city has been blended into a fantasia at once logical and agreeable.

Apart from the cosmopolitan scope of architectural motifs, the architecture of the exposition reveals, in the main, two stylistic trends—traditional and contemporary. Although the plan exhibits academic concepts of order, alike monumental and impressive, and although the architecture also profusely acknowledges its indebtedness to the past, nevertheless, within the general scheme many striking and aesthetically satisfactory units in the idiom of today are incorporated. Both past and present have been given full scope for expression by the simple device of separate unit arrangements in terms of self-contained enclosed courts joined by stylistically neutral intermediaries, or frankly separated by open natural areas. With some minor exceptions, the "modernistic" cubistic extravagances and vagaries of the Chicago fair of 1933 and the projected "utopian" style of the New York fair are here conspicuous by their absence.

In order to assist the layman—and this book is for the layman—to appreciate the apparent but not really conflicting aims and ideals of traditional and contemporary architecture, it may be well here to summarize briefly the more basic philosophies which operate in the two schools.

The conservative traditionalist or academic architect, when wholly a reactionary, is satisfied to borrow ideas and forms from the past. He relies primarily upon his indispensable library of copybooks, which he keeps at his elbow. Since he is unable or unwilling to think independently, he copies, relying upon the past to carry him to success, and not realizing that the excellence of this glorious past is the result of a process primarily creative and not imitative. The world has many architects of this type; their works are only too common. They can

16

THE ARCH OF THE WINDS AS SEEN FROM THE COURT OF REFLECTIONS

hardly be regarded as artists, and while at best they possess impressive knowledge, they make no contribution of their own and their work is likely to be commonplace, dry, uninteresting, and without sustaining vitality.

The creative scholarly architect, on the contrary, uses the past not as an end in itself, but as a source of inspiration for his own creative processes in solving the architectural problems of his own time. Blessed with imagination, he is able to reformulate the past in new patterns and new formal relationships. This kind of artist has given to the world significant architecture in the past, and we may be sure that he will continue to do so in the future. Of this type of architecture, the product of architects who combine scholarship with creative ability, the Exposition has abundant examples.

The "modern" architect also uses the elements of the past, particularly those of structure—there is no escape from them—but, for aesthetic, economic, material, or other reasons, he has developed his own spatial and decorative features out of the material and the conditions of his time. The rejection of mechanically produced ornamentation endlessly and thoughtlessly repeated, ornament which has not grown out of the structure or function of the material of a building, is typical of the "modern" architect. He creatively expresses, as did the Greeks, or the Italians of the Renaissance, the spirit of his own era in his own way. His work is, in large measure, an honest expression of a scientific-mechanistic civilization—of its speed, efficiency, economy, hygienic requirements, and others of its typical qualities.

There is also the "modernistic" or pseudo-modern architect—happily, with some minor exceptions, barred from Treasure Island—who, either lost in the bewilderments of an era of transition, or suffering from a sense of futility, revels in all sorts of ideas that are merely "different" or bizarre. He is likely to carry to the most illogical conclusion such slogans as "Form follows function." He is often bedeviled by modern materials—reinforced concrete, glass, chromium steel—and by gadgets and "accessories." In his obvious efforts to bowl you over he is not incomparable in his methods to the shock troops of modern armies;

19

and his like is to be found in other contemporary artistic activities. He is often merely sensational, primarily seeking to attract attention at any price; but what remains, after the first impact, is often disappointing, puerile, futile, and lacking in spiritual values—in fact, it is often inhuman. He is the proud apostle of chaos and of an alleged disintegration of society and life in general. He may startle us, but he cannot deceive us; his work is not likely to stand the test of time.

But let us examine what is actually shown.

An inspection of the architecture of the Exposition may appropriately begin with the main or Pacific gate, which faces west upon the broad expanse of the Marina and looks toward San Francisco. The effect of this striking architectural aggregate is "modern" in the best sense. In its massive strength, in its rhythmically measured uplift of terraced shapes reflecting ancient Mayan structures, it is as "classical" as the Tower of Babel or the Pyramids. Surmounted as it is by the rugged forms of gigantic elephants, its effect is imposing, monumental, and decorative. People always on the alert for symbolic meanings have attributed to these severely stylized beasts various meanings, even of political significance. I am confident that such implications were not intended by the designer, and I feel sure that the use of these massive shapes is a result of the architect's and sculptor's conviction that they would lend themselves particularly well to architectural and sculptural purposes. The desired shapes might have been derived from any other animal form if it had been endowed with the same architectonic, plastic prerequisites.

Within the terraced walls of this gateway, great verticals present themselves, overlapping as they recede inward, accelerating one's steps by their rhythmical formula. On closer approach, they reveal a broad opening which allows one to pass obliquely into a plain and restricted intermediate court gayly accentuated with colorful decorative maps (Born). From here one enters the great central court, the Court of Honor, which is at once dignified and impressive, reflecting that serenity of spirit which is the imperishable legacy of the Greeks. It is dominated by the physically most imposing feature of the Exposition, the

IN THE COURT OF REFLECTIONS

Tower of the Sun. Although the court itself is circular in design, the tower is octagonal, tapering into a pyramidal point surmounted by a gigantic Phoenix.

Because towers are conspicuous they naturally come in for much criticism, and the Tower of the Sun has already had its share of this, particularly from critics who insist upon novelty. It is apparent that the tower is not directly reminiscent of any historical type, but is freely created in the spirit of tradition modified by personal ideas. In its emphasis of strong verticals it possesses a marked sense of uplift—a most desirable attribute in any tower. The so-called "Tower of Jewels" of the 1915 exposition, with its monotonous piling up of alternating drums and cubes and its repetitive emphasis of heavy horizontal lines, defeated itself and at best was a gigantic but static pile, lifeless and inanimate. Even the twinkling "jewels" of Bohemian colored glass could not give any spark of life to that dead colossus. It is undeniable that the Exposition tower on Treasure Island has both great dignity and, in its rhythmical space division, its tall open arches, great charm. From a distance it has much of the quality of a gigantic shaft, carrying more lasting appeal than the purely sensational "trylon" which dominates the New York fair. Of course, the "trylon"—a triangular obelisk— standing alongside a great "perisphere" is unusually striking because of its enormous size, but reduced to the dimensions of a small picture it certainly cannot boast originality of design; its originality rests solely in its colossal scale.

A special feature of the central court is four belvederes or loggias, each with a great elliptical opening in its ceiling, called the oculus, which permits the visitor to glance upward into the open sky. These enclosed and lofty spaces primarily offer shelter and convenient vantage points from which one may observe the handsomely landscaped court and the tower. The center of each belvedere is emphasized by a symbolic statue, of which more will be said in the next chapter.

To the south, one enters the Court of the Moon and Stars (Kelham), guarded at its southern entrance by two towerlike structures which terminate in rhythmically receding setbacks. The architecture of this court is frankly eclectic and is perhaps derived from too many divergent sources of the traditional classical sort. The crenelated cornice, suggesting medieval military architecture, is foreign to its generally playful and fragile character. Its chief qualities are intimacy and refinement, and a certain delicacy suggested by its name is reflected in its perhaps too generously used surface ornamentation. A long basin arched by its jets of water and flanked by numerous urns and stately yews, gives this court a decidedly decorative quality.

From the Court of the Moon and Stars and toward Yerba Buena Island one looks into a sunken area, the Enchanted Garden, with its luxuriance of trees, shrubs, and flowers, of which more will be said in another chapter.

Near by, to the east of the Enchanted Garden and overlooking it, stands the plain and deliberately utilitarian structure erected by the womens' clubs and called the Yerba Buena Clubhouse (Wurster). This building has an attraction that results from an intelligently applied economy of means. "Modern" in its rejection of meaningless ornamentation, it achieves an ingratiating appearance, gay and appealing. Its walled courtyard, the lattice-covered walls of which carry vines, lend it the character of a secluded suburban residence. Its unpretentious exterior gives no hint of the elaborate decorative scheme which has been evolved inside.

Three other buildings on the southern side of the island engage one's attention, if only by their size. These somewhat sober structures are the Administration Building, situated near the causeway, and two low buildings which readily suggest by their peculiar shape their ultimate use as aviation hangars. All three of these buildings are permanent and intended for government use after the Exposition shall have vanished. Although not designed for an exposition fiesta, they have been usefully and fairly effectively drawn into the temporary service of the enterprise.

The Administration Building, with its hospitable, embracing, semicircular ground plan, is not without formal distinction. The two aviation buildings in their massive simplicity and low, earth-hugging

24

THE COURT OF FLOWERS, WITH THE RAINBOW FOUNTAIN

shapes suggest little more than shelter and protection, and that is, indeed, both their present and their ultimate purpose. In fact, the one nearest the Yerba Buena Clubhouse contains a display of aviation equipment. The one farther to the east has been temporarily enlarged and ingeniously fitted out to house a representative display in the special field of the fine and applied arts; here, Occident and Orient, their pictorial expressions as well as their plastic arts, and their crafts both ancient and modern, have been combined under one roof into an impressive spectacle such as the West has never before had an opportunity to enjoy.

To the east of the central court, two courts separated from each other by a high arch continue the architectural scheme. Both of these courts are designed in a modified traditional style faintly suggesting Gothic and Renaissance influences. Both were designed by the same architect (Hobart). Being almost completely enclosed on all four sides, their attraction is in their well-calculated simplicity. The arch that divides them is monumental in proportions, reaching high into space; ostensibly it belongs to another world.

The long, rectangular court adjoining the central court is called the Court of Reflections and, as its name suggests, derives much of its appeal from two long, rectangular pools and profuse horticultural embellishments and accents, which have resulted in an effective contrast of architectural form and the accents furnished by the landscape designer. Passing through the triumphal arch, one enters the nearly square Court of Flowers, which also is designed in an architectural style eclectically derived from historic sources but simplified so as to bring it close in spirit to the economy of means so characteristic of contemporary architecture. In the center of this court is a terraced pool, circular in shape, decorated by sculptural figures of aquatic origin, and surmounted by a figure symbolizing a rainbow; and in the four corners of the court, secondary basins add to its interest. With its arcade it is particularly gay; and it is luxuriant in its wealth of foliage, of a great variety of natural forms and colors, and lively with its constant play of water.

The eastern terminus of the Court of Flowers is a set of two tower-like structures called Temples of the East. Their masses and decorative details are mainly of Asiatic inspiration; the crowning motif more particularly is inspired by the processional umbrellas of Siam. These towers with their playful quality of imaginative fancy reflect both learning and feeling, qualities essential to good architecture. Their great architectural bases are designed as semicircular steps similar to those which along the Ganges in India are crowded with bathers and used as cremation sites. Perhaps unaware of their original uses, Exposition visitors come here to recover from the extended walks which expositions entail, and to enjoy a view, from a higher elevation, of the great lagoon with its many enchanting reflections, or to let their eyes wander toward the eastern shore of the Bay.

These two beehive-shaped towers are particularly successful as exposition architecture. They are playful and imaginative, both in form and in color. Their frank indebtedness to Oriental motives seems very appropriate in view of the theme of the Exposition, which stresses the cultural and artistic achievements of many countries and races living on the shores of the Pacific Ocean. They form an architectural bridge to the buildings in the near-by areas to the north and east that represent Asiatic countries. These will be discussed later.

Returning to the central court, one sees to the north a long impressive enclosure which assumes the character of a *via trimphalis* set with great standards and lanterns, a great boulevard rather than a court, open on the north and ending in the monumental Court of the Pacific. This connecting great Court of the Seven Seas is suggestive of travel and adventure. Its architect (Kelham) has shown resourcefulness in the use of the tradition in which it is conceived, for some of its many embellishments are distinctive and decoratively most effective, reflecting the fertility of the Renaissance. The court derives its special character from an architectural and sculptural motive, the prow of a galley terminating in the shape of a winged figure. At sixteen intervals this motive appears again and again, projecting from the great pylons that divide the enclosing mass of buildings, and the reiteration does not

A FOUNTAIN IN THE COURT OF FLOWERS

result in an unpleasant mechanical effect, but rather gives the suggestion of a fleet of many ships which sail the seven seas, each bent upon adventure and discovery.

The Court of the Seven Seas opens, at the north, into a great court once projected as the Court of the Four Hemispheres but eventually modified into the Court of Pacifica. People who think of the Pacific Ocean in terms of tranquillity had best ignore this misleading although generally accepted designation, and think of it as the "great ocean," and in that way will better appreciate the creation of the architect (Pflueger). Vast it is, imposing in scale, of a massive simplicity which, so to speak, sets an emotional pace for itself—a quality discernible also in others of Mr. Pflueger's contributions to the Exposition, for example, the Federal Building and the façade of the California Building. Its impressiveness arises first of all from its colossal scale, which one appreciates on comparing its actual size with that of other units of the Exposition and with the inevitable measuring stick, the human being. Its effective use of "modern" architectural ideas is immediately apparent; that is, the aesthetic qualities it produces result from the use of pure plastic form unadorned by superimposed traditional decorative forms. Here are carefully calculated vertical and horizontal surfaces effectively interrelated, resolving themselves into strikingly interesting contrasts of light and shade, which give to the whole a stately, even austere, simplicity and grandeur. The main decorative plastic feature of this court is the gigantic figure of Pacifica, clearly visible at a great distance as one approaches it from the south.

This completes an analysis of the main, or better perhaps, official group of buildings; but connected with these we have still to consider a number of architectural units of no less importance, most of them created along an extension of the east-west axis toward the eastern side of the island.

Looking out of the Court of Flowers over the waters of the great lagoon, one sees inescapably the gigantic, somewhat gaunt structure of the Federal Building. This building, at first glance unorthodox, is reminiscent of a classic peristyle, and as such it functions in the simplest and most economical structural terms, and is stately, imposing, impressive, commensurate with the dignity and power of the government of a great nation. As a candid departure from the official architecture of Washington it could hardly go farther; but such comparisons are futile. Considered as a separate architectural unit, it indelibly impresses itself upon the visitor. Not only stylistically, but also in terms of its material, it is to be labeled truly "modern," being more nearly honest and rational than exposition architecture generally can afford to be with its simulation of permanent stone made of wood and stucco. The frank and undisguised use of steel, wood, and other modern materials successfully exploited for decorative effects resulting from structural function, is one of the interesting and impressive qualities of the Federal Building. Its commanding central feature is an open colonnade of timberwork columns, four abreast, twelve in a row, symbolizing the forty-eight states of the Union. Sky and water and distant shoreland are effectively drawn into this inspiring structure, thus adding the softening touch of nature.

Flanking the Federal Building on either side, and composed so as to supplement it and to set it off, are groups of buildings facing a spacious, tree-lined, open court east of the great lagoon, called the Court of the Nation. These were contributed by the state of California, its many counties, and the city of San Francisco. To insure harmony with the central Federal Building and a proper setting for it, the design of these façades was also given over to the control of Mr. Pflueger. The California and San Francisco buildings (on the right) and the auditorium (on the left) are not unlike the Federal Building in concept, but less formidable than the structure symbolizing the dignity and strength of an entire nation.

In connection with the California Building—that is to say, to the rear of it—the counties of the State have been grouped and tied together into architectural units as single neighborly groups of counties of common interest, reflecting, as in the Redwood Empire Building, the natural and physical resources of several counties together. Here is the Shasta-Cascade Building, the Alameda-Contra Costa Building,

ENTRANCE TO THE COURT OF FLOWERS, WITH TALL BAMBOO AND ARALIA

and other county-group structures farther to the rear and south. In fact, the several county groups have all made a definite contribution architecturally. Many diversified elements have been well tied together into a lively decorative pattern of modern architectural form often gay in design and color and decidedly "expositional" in effect.

To the north of the Federal Building a classical structure, dignified but not without distinction, enclosing a great court, accommodates the western states. To the north of it, Missouri convincingly demonstrates its traditional imperviousness to outside authority. Illinois also is satisfied to present itself in a building dignified enough but hardly exciting.

From the spacious open area in front of the Federal Building so aptly called the Court of the Nation, and in a northerly and easterly direction, there is visible a complex of buildings dominated by the so-called "theme building" of the exposition. Here Pacific House (Merchant) stands on an island approached from the east by an arched bridge suggestive of Oriental influences. Pacific House, the social and cultural center of this international area, is conspicuous for its extremely simple, well-proportioned masses and its equally simple decorative elements developed entirely from the structural function of the window openings. These strong vertical lines give it dignity, and its picturesque situation, surrounded by water, gives it an advantage not possessed by any other building in the Exposition ensemble; it seems, indeed, designed for its pictorial effectiveness as reflected in the surrounding waters. It is a handsome structure both within and without, and richly repays frequent visits.

In this vicinity are also many more or less informally arranged buildings and pavilions representing distant lands of the Pacific Basin—Japan, the Dutch East Indies, Johore, New Zealand, Australia, and French Indo-China; and of course Hawaii and the Philippines. And near by is the Latin-American Court, where the pavilions of Mexico, El Salvador, Costa Rica, Panama, Guatemala, Ecuador, Peru, Colombia, and Chile are combined in one picturesque aggregate which reflects the ancient architectural heritage of those countries.

Japan particularly, again as in 1915, charms by the consistent application of a kind of beauty typical of this ancient nation since time immemorial. Craftsmanship and good taste, the love of the Japanese for small things, are blended here in the creation of an architectural ensemble representing the estate of a Japanese noble, and a connected shrine, racial throughout in its flavor. It is the Japan of a people living in close union with Nature, listening to her voice, enchanted by her beauty, a beauty recaptured in the beauty of the buildings and the garden area enclosing a picturesque pool. The great wealth of natural beauty revealed here in a relatively small area is amazing, and although the effect in many ways is monumental, its intimacy and the persistent beauty of even the smallest detail reflect at every turn the age-old regard of the Japanese for skill as a means toward the creating of beautiful major and minor forms.

North of it and balancing it on the intersection of the Western Way and the Pacific Promenade, the building of the Dutch East Indies, adapted from an ancient Hindu Javanese temple, artistically holds its own alongside the Japanese Building. Its characteristically Javanese architecture, culminating in a beautifully proportioned tower, is another one of the fascinating pieces of architecture on Treasure Island. Like the Japanese Building, it excels in the use of intricate and decorative sculptural detail. The Johore Building, not far away, is a replica of a native Malay house with its steeply sloping roof and ornamented eaves, picturesquely situated on a small peninsula; and across the water New Zealand leans upon its primitive heritage of the Maoris.

Italy, Brazil, the Argentine Republic, and France, on the west side of the Pacific Promenade, house themselves in buildings essentially in the modern idiom such as recent expositions in Europe have so effectively cultivated. Rather than symbolizing power of state or cultural traditions by resurrecting historic edifices burdened with bombastic ornament, these buildings achieve a new kind of beauty, simple, refreshing, effective in the honest use of contemporary materials. For Argentina and Brazil, historically new countries, this was less of a problem; but even in the pavilions of Italy and France, nations that are treasure houses of classical art, the modern spirit prevails. These buildings possess the undeniable decorative effectiveness that results from structural elements developed as decorative forms. Plain vertical and horizontal surfaces, gayly colored bold silhouettes of form, give to them all a high degree of gaiety and vitality. The pavilions of Argentina and Brazil emphasize in their decorative ideas the natural beauty and agricultural resources of those countries; those of Italy and France reflect the high artistic standards which those nations have achieved in the fine as well as the applied arts.

It is not possible to account here for every structure on Treasure Island that merits attention for artistic reasons, but among several others the Temple of Religion (Bolles) and the pavilion of Christian Science Activities may be mentioned. Although the Hall of Religion suggests Gothic influences, both these structures in the main reflect the contemporary spirit in architecture. Apart from these, numerous utilitarian buildings—restaurants, cafés, kiosks, bridges—reflect the guiding hand of the several architects who so ably created the artistic values of the Exposition.

Chapter III

THE SCULPTURE

SCULPTURE and architecture are two arts held together by the closest kinship. Both deal with the same materials—stone, wood, metal, terra cotta, and concrete. Architecture usually finds expression in abstract forms; sculpture is more generally concerned with representative forms, particularly the human figure. Both arts naturally profit from this kinship. Architecture by the use of sculptural adornments may through them reveal the human purposes which a building is to satisfy. Even more important is the contribution of sculpture to architecture in enriching surfaces, softening transitions, and reducing angularity. It may even contribute to the organic strength of a structure; so, for example, serve the gigantic elephants at the west gate of the Exposition.

Of course, there are legitimate and important uses to which sculpture may be put besides the decoration of buildings and the adornment of parks. Sculpture when used indoors may more intimately represent a person, tell a story, illustrate some historic event. But if it is to survive, it must also meet artistic responsibilities. In the present enterprise our first concern is with what is called architectural sculpture, that is, sculpture used out of doors as an integral part of a large and complex architectural scheme. Sculpture of this type is itself a gainer when so used.

It is doubtless true that architectural monumental sculpture sacrifices something of its freedom and perhaps also of its intimacy of feeling when it assumes the rôle of a collaborator, but it is in accommodating this restriction that sculptors have often disclosed their real talents. The sculptor conscious of the highest aims of his art is never happier than when he is called upon to decorate a public building not in terms of a portrait bust in the foyer, but in grand-scale figural embellishment as part of a monumental architectural setting. It is under these conditions that he can best demonstrate his creative ability and give the fullest account of the mastery of his material and of the tools of his craft.

Although at the exposition of 1915 our western architects more than held their own in competition with their eastern colleagues, almost all the sculpture—with some few but creditable exceptions—was done by men and women from the East. Doubtless in 1914 we were not ready to wrestle successfully with the problems of monumental architectural sculpture. The large artistic demonstrations of visiting sculptors in 1915 undoubtedly had, however, the effect of challenging the ambitions of the westerners, and we are now in a position to see how this challenge has been met. Moreover, nearly twenty-five years have passed since the Panama-Pacific International Exposition, and a new generation of sculptors has grown up—both in years and in skill—on the Pacific Coast.

It may be said at the start that most of our sculptors give a good account of themselves. It must be clear, also, in comparison with other artists represented, that the sculptor's contribution to the Exposition is not alone the determining factor in its extraordinary artistic effectiveness. The credit here must go also to the architect, the horticulturist, the director of color, and the illuminating expert. One thing we can safely say for the work of most of our sculptors is that it is characterized by independent thinking, artistic courage, even a spirit of adventure, although it may not always be technically adequate. Inevitably there are in evidence ideas inappropriate or not properly realized—even ineffective. The enormous scale of our Exposition obviously presented a problem which the sculptors who were accustomed to think in studio terms were not always able to meet. Sculpture conceived and developed under the limitations of a studio may often reveal itself as inadequate when placed out of doors against monumental, large-scale architecture.

40

THE TOWERS OF THE EAST

It will be remembered that in 1915 there was employed a director of sculpture who was entrusted with the supervision of all sculptural work. This time, a supervising director of sculpture has been dispensed with, and each architect has been given a free hand in selecting his own sculptural collaborators from the available local colony. This broad and sensible policy seems justified by the absence of the stereotyped work that is always likely to result from the domination of a single point of view. Since the architecture of the Exposition expresses stylistic tendencies from the classical to the modern idiom in pure and functional form, a variety of sculptural modes have required to be called into being to harmonize with individual architectural units.

The Panama-Pacific International Exposition was a child of a period of affluence; its economic background was the accumulation of prolonged national prosperity. In 1915 a great deal of money was available, and a great deal was spent, sometimes for its own sake, and the presence of a piece of sculpture in many a nook and corner of the exposition of that year could only be explained by the prevailing affluence of the time. The present Exposition has felt, as have many other enterprises, the restraining hand of economy. What may at first, however, appear to have been a handicap upon the art of the Exposition, has actually, and beneficially, prevented a wholesale display of meretricious carving.

But let us get down to particulars. Our examination of the sculpture may be carried out in the same order as was our view of the architecture; and this scheme will be followed.

Short of an occasional decorative detail, no sculptural material is to be found anywhere on or against the severely simple western walls of the Exposition, for its use has been in large measure limited to the courts within the walled and sheltered city. Inasmuch as the outside shell, at least on the west and north, mainly serves the purpose of creating shelter, anything as engaging as a work of storytelling sculpture requiring prolonged attention seemed unjustified there. The enclosed courts, then, are the backgrounds against which sculpture has been displayed effectively and in an adequate amount.

43

The first real impact with sculpture, and it is a mighty one, is with the colossal forms of the elephants on the outside of the two towers flanking the west gate. Since early times, the elephant has held an important place in pageantry, processions, and public ceremonials. Its great physical bulk, its formidable strength, its stately dignity have lent impressiveness to many historic occasions. As a symbol of Asia it seems as appropriate to the theme of the Pacific pageant as would the buffalo to a theme purely American, and, transformed and greatly simplified into decorative forms, it produces an effect both dignified and impressive. The "elephant towers" will be long remembered by all visitors to the Exposition.

The question has been asked, Is this architecture or sculpture? The dividing line here is indeed hard to draw. The forms were designed as an integral part of the architecture, but the actual shaping was the result of a sculptor's labor (Macky). The creative collaboration between architect and sculptor was so very close that the acceptance of a joint authorship is inevitable.

The great Court of Honor, dominated by the Tower of the Sun, contains numerous sculptural works of the detached, free-standing type, and others that are integrated into the architectural surfaces. Within the four belvederes are placed single figures, symbolizing Fauna, Flora, Land, and Sea. Although they are the separate works of four artists, they are held together by a quality of restraint that is at once classical and pleasing. Mr. Malmquist is the author of Fauna, Mr. Cadorin modeled Land, Mr. Puccinelli contributed the figure of Flora, and the Sea is from the hand of Carlo Taliabue. Malmquist and Taliabue have in common a stylistically severe treatment of line that is architecturally very effective, whereas Cadorin and Puccinelli depend upon the softer forms reminiscent of actuality. The work of the latter two is perhaps the more ingratiating, but it lacks somewhat in architectural strength. All four statues have been effectively treated to resemble bronze and thus form a striking accent and are at the same time kept visually within the enclosed space in which they are displayed.

A TOWER OF THE EAST AS SEEN ACROSS THE LAGOON

High up over the broadly arched west walls are two reclining figures, symbolizing Air and Water (Kent). There is an eerie quality about these figures that gives them the appearance of floating in space rather than being part of a wall. Although, in comparison with other sculptural works in the Court of Honor, they lack in technical sophistication, their evanescent quality is most ingratiating—not unlike that of the figures in paintings by John Carroll. They are more like a passing vision than a fixed sculptural decoration in the conventional sense, and they fascinate by their very unconventionality and daring.

As a part of the tower, Mr. Gordon Huff here contributed the models for four figures representing Industry, Agriculture, Science, and the Arts. These stand on high pedestals in the tower's tall, open arches. One must note that although Mr. Huff's work is sound, and rich in craftsmanship, it is somewhat lacking in inspiration. It is dignified but not dynamic, pleasing rather than stimulating. His scale and craftsmanship seem adequate to the requirements of the tower, and the opulent quality of these statues adds a sense of richness to the sober architectural surfaces of the tower structure.

Of Malmquist's numerous contributions to the Exposition sculpture, several are found in the central court. His Phoenix, a gigantic fabulous creature twenty feet high, surmounts the great tower. Its somewhat complicated design is not entirely intelligible from the great distance from which it necessarily must be seen. However, since a Phoenix is a product of the imagination, a sculptor may well shape it to suit his own fancy; and that is what Malmquist has done. Its tantalizing, involved, somewhat baroque outline arouses one's curiosity concerning what it may mean, and people have taken the Phoenix for a variety of things: a gigantic insect, or an eagle, or a mighty winged victory. After all, what the Phoenix means to the intellect is here unimportant. As a gilded finial of magnificent proportions it soars like a great flame into space, suggesting infinity and unrestricted power.

Below the spire are the appropriate minor sculptural accents of the head of a lion repeated on the eight vertical planes of the tower. Above the tall slender arches, high up, are four reliefs (Malmquist) which are repeated to cover the same eight planes. These represent gentle and cold winds, trade winds, and storms. They reveal to a marked degree the work of the experienced architectural sculptor. The technical preciseness and definiteness leave, however, little to the imagination, and in spite of their positive qualities they are too vague to be properly effective at the great height at which they are placed. Over the four arched entrances to the tower, at its base, are decorative designs from the signs of the zodiac, similar to the wind designs, but more effective in their lower position because they are more accessible to the eye. Apart from engaging the intellect, they add a surface accent at a point where it seems most welcome.

On the east wall of this court, over the two side doors leading into the Court of Reflections, two panels of kneeling figures (Slivka) have been inserted. These two panels, representing Fertility and Abundance, are in a modified classical style. Their sensitive linear design and clear pattern are quite in keeping with their architectural setting.

The Court of the Moon and Stars holds Cadorin's statue of the Star Maiden, ensconced upon a fountain—a naturalistic, pretty, somewhat coquettish figure at once ingratiating and coyly sentimental. Although we have long since ceased to be moved by sculpture of this type, the public choice will probably place it high on the preferred list of Exposition carving.

This court abounds in a great deal of surface ornamentation and decoration (Tognelli) that is in some degree in keeping with the playful, festive character of the setting. It adds little to the structural effectiveness of the architecture, but is used rather to illustrate literary ideas sustaining the fanciful character of the area. The subject-matter is derived from many sources, all fanciful, romantic, and appealing to the imagination. The stories of Saint George and the Dragon, Aladdin and the Wonderful Lamp, Achilles and the Centaur, the Moon Princess, Prince Igor, Jack and the Beanstalk—all these and more make a veritable picture book of this court. Several of them are done in a simple, unobtrusive, incised relief, and where these are

PROWS OF GALLEYS IN THE COURT OF THE SEVEN SEAS

placed between niches and over recessed doorways they are not conspicuous, being often screened by shrubbery. It is only of those in the corner towers—the South Towers—that one becomes unduly conscious. In spite of interesting and admirable detail in these sculptured stories, the great assembly of ornament generally employed makes the total effect, particularly in the towers, pretentious and distracting.

In the spacious garden south of the Court of the Moon and Stars, Haig Patigian has contributed four standing figures, Earth Dormant, Sunshine, Rain, and Harvest. The scale of these dignified figures seems adequate to a setting lacking in any dominating architectural structure, and the conscious simplification of the draperies and accessories of the standing figures has resulted in effective outdoor sculpture. The figures impress by their classical dignity and seem appropriate to an area given over to recreation and quiet contemplation. In this neighborhood, Cadorin's Moon and the Dawn plays its part in the general mood of the area.

In the eastern long court, the Court of Reflections, the only sculpture is found in deeply recessed hexagonal panels (Meyer). These compositions, called Beauty, Knowledge, Music, and Labor, are repeated alternately, high on the walls of the court, and serve as much the purpose of an accent as that of conveying an idea. Above them the cornice with its repeated indentations and perforations creates a feeling of animation that contrasts happily with the forthright simplicity of this court and its spirit of peace and tranquillity. Here also may be seen Edgar Walter's pleasing figure of the Penguin Girl. Although not originally designed for this setting, it has been happily placed at the end of one of the two long basins. It stands as a reminder of this very talented sculptor, a good citizen, and loyal friend, whose recent untimely death brought general regret to his native city. The two highly stylized eagles on the great arch are the work of Schnier, who here subordinated himself completely to architecture so that a recognizable personal style did not assert itself; that is to say, the eagles might have been done by anyone. Still, they function well structurally both in scale and in form. In this court, unlike the others, no fountains distract the surfaces of the placid pools, which spread through its entire length, reflecting in their mirrorlike surfaces many alluring pictures of architectural forms mingled with luxuriant planting.

The adjoining square, the Court of Flowers, is dominated by a fountain in which stands Malmquist's graceful figure of The Rainbow. Malmquist's self-assured, well-disciplined style is here again easily recognizable; his work everywhere gives the impression that he is never in doubt of what is effective in a work of sculpture, and that he unhesitatingly follows his convictions. The meaning of the symbolic statue is clear, its scale is adequate, and its decorative effectiveness is marked; it only lacks that freedom which leaves a little to the imagination. The tall shaft on which the figure stands is somewhat alien in character stylistically, beckoning to the ornate Temples of the East just outside.

The several human and animal aquatic figures engaged in a playful tussle about the edges of the circular central basin are imaginative, and are decorative in their effect. The four corners of this court are emphasized by four elevated secondary fountains, each containing an ornate decorative head contrasting with the clear forms of the architecture of this lively and stimulating garden court.

Just to the east, outside this court, are two great sculptured panels done in low relief. The one on the right is by Schnier, that on the left by Braghetta. Their function is to enliven great wall panels, and they do this admirably.

In Schnier's Dance of Life this sculptor's capacity for decorative values is well and consistently revealed on a very large scale. Every detail of his sprightly theme has been carefully explored for decoratively effective forms, nothing has been left to accident, and the consistently applied process of simplification has added clarity and decorative effectiveness to the gigantic panel, the gold finish of which adds greatly to the clearness of its linear design. It is one of the most effective sculptures of this type in the Exposition, both for its decorative effectiveness and precision of style and for the fascination of its subject-matter.

THE COURT OF PACIFICA

53

Miss Braghetta's panel, Path of Darkness, is at first glance stylistically a mate to Schnier's. On closer study, it is seen to lack the firmly architectural quality that is characteristic of Schnier's work. It suffers from the use of too many slumping, curvilinear forms; in other words, it is a little soft in design. And this is by no means the fault of the theme. Compare the cloud forms in the right-hand panel with those in the left. The former, Schnier's, have a self-sustained, structural quality; Miss Braghetta's are forms with two dimensions only. The repetition of the drooping position of the heads in the left-hand panel is overdone; it is repetitious without that sense of invention which relieves repeated ideas from monotony. In Schnier's panels there is variety within harmony, a quality that gives interest to any work of art.

We must now retrace our steps to the Court of the Seven Seas. Here, as in the Court of the Moon and Stars, all the decorative sculptural work was done by Tognelli. His work, as we have seen before, has all the dexterity and decorative playfulness of the experienced architectural sculptor. His fondness for skill leaves little room for emotional values. All his work is decorative rather than expressive; but that is a quality legitimate enough in exposition ornamentation. Many historical themes are here carved into walls and niches, and the intellect is as much engaged as the eye. Man's conquests of the oceans of the world are incised in many panels, and ships and the sea play an important part in the scheme of decoration.

Exploration, trade, and commerce are the leitmotifs in this great court dedicated to adventure and travel. High up on the equally spaced sixty-foot pylons is repeated the decorative and bold form of the prow of a galley, graced by a winged figure representing the spirit of adventure. This architectural sculptural decoration seen in strong profile against the sky is advantageously placed and very effective. In the center of this court is Patigian's composite group, Creation, a little irrelevant to the environment. Its soft forms recall his fondness for classical sources.

From here one enters the spacious north court, the Court of Pacifica, dominated by the physically biggest sculptural work at the Exposi-

55

tion, the gigantic statue of Pacifica. Its eighty-foot height rises majestically in front of a metal curtain in front of the north wall of the court. Mr. Stackpole must derive some quiet satisfaction from recalling to himself that in 1915 his charming, rather sentimental, little kneeling figure enshrined before the Palace of Fine Arts was probably the least conspicuous, perhaps even the smallest, outdoor figure at the fair. This time, his heroic Pacifica is the largest and most conspicuous single unit in the entire Exposition.

Although its symbolism may not be quite clear, one must admire its decorative effectiveness. The spiritual quality that made itself felt in an early small model—a suggestion of the mystery that is associated with the Orient—has not been entirely retained in the final cast. Because of that lack of an inner meaning, the statue has little more than architectural effectiveness, not unlike that of the elephants at the west gate. Some of its minor forms possess a baroque quality rather foreign to the generally severe architecture of the court, and these, particularly in the arms, are so arbitrary that they interfere with the intelligibility of the figure without exerting other and compensating qualities. The decoratively effective curtain of metal stars and small tubes forms a sort of backdrop behind Pacifica. Under certain weather conditions they were to produce melodious sounds—like the "singing" statue of Memnon?—but our languorous climate, unwilling to play its part, had to be assisted mechanically.

Surrounding the terraced fountain in the center of this majestic court, the works of eight sculptors compete with one another in a variety of figures representing peoples living on the shores of the Pacific Ocean. It is not often that eight artists of differing artistic temper are invited to share the responsibility for so closely united a structure as this fountain. The difficulties resulting are obvious at a glance, and the problem of an objective critical estimate is further complicated by the unusual circumstance that the twelve figures of the inside are the work of four women sculptors, and the four pairs of figures surrounding them are the work of four men. Perhaps a mere catalogue description of these figures in terms of their titles would be the simplest escape

56

SAN FRANCISCO BUILDING

from the dilemma, but one must choose to face the issue as one sees it. Certainly these twenty figures are the work of artists of a wide range of ideas, technical experience, and ability; but it seems that those who appear to be the better grounded in the technique of their craft are perhaps the less satisfactory in performance—their work shows the least amount of adventurous spirit, whereas the others, handicapped by apparent technical inexpertness, have taken on responsibilities too ambitious for their professional equipment.

Here is Schnier, the able craftsman once more, with two reclining figures abounding in suave, rhythmical forms representing the quiet, inward-looking spirit of India. Schnier always goes unfalteringly for his clearly seen objective; nothing is left to accident. The pose is unconventional and casual; the expression mysterious, even enigmatic. Altogether, it is a competent and effective work of its particular type, in excellent taste; its only lack is in freedom.

Balancing Schnier's figures on the east side are two seated figures by George, one representing a native American, the other a modern American woman. Compared with Schnier's, these figures obviously lack an expert handling of the material; they show no finesse whatever. As designs, they are frankly conventional. Diagonally across are two Polynesian figures by Carlton. Although sculpture is often most effective when representing figures in repose, this element here has become a static quality.

In the outer circle, on the southeast corner Johnson has ingeniously put two Inca Indians astride of llamas. Llamas can't be ridden, in actuality; but that fact is not necessarily relevant to art. These compositions, so very unconventional, do not lack the merit of artistic invention. However, their design pattern sets them radically apart from their neighbors.

We must now approach the inner circle formed by the ladies. One of the best things one can say about these striking bits of artistic adventure is that one feels oneself inescapably drawn to them. That all four groups are full of ideas, no one would deny. They certainly are not trite, commonplace, or stereotyped—they are teeming with vitality, insistently so in some aspects. Among them, moreover, is one of the finest pieces of plastic art which the Exposition offers out of doors; that is Miss Kent's statue, Young Man Improvising Music. A little more attention to technically refined execution would have added to the clarity of this effective and appealing work. It possesses both outer form and an inner life. It is more than decorative. Her two accompanying figures of girls resting and listening are too distorted to explain themselves satisfactorily, although in their strained postures they emphasize the repose of the central figure of this group.

Miss Graham's adventure into the realm of monumental sculpture on the opposite (east) side is a courageous attempt to avoid hackneyed ideas, but she goes perhaps too far. Her central figure is excellent, though technically a little careless in execution; it will do for Exposition sculpture, though it would never in its crude state be satisfactory as a permanent embellishment of a public park. The two side figures are illustrative rather than effective as plastic embellishments. Seen from certain viewpoints, the figures are so unconventional as to invite being taken unseriously.

Miss Phillips's group is surmounted by a male figure clashing cymbals and flanked on one side by a female figure of a flutist and on the other by a second female figure blowing a horn. This work is rich in moving planes and decorative forms, but rather involved and confused, particularly the two lower kneeling figures. The side figures of Ruth Cravath's group are not altogether satisfactory, for similar reasons, although her central figure is an excellent piece of sculpture.

One cannot help but feel that the four central figures in the inner circle are more successful than their accompanying side figures. In their totality they all play a part in adding to the lively and exotic spirit of the fountain; but they do not make for an agreeable unity. The general result of this composite undertaking would have been more satisfactory if objective representation had been merely tempered by subjective expression. Ours is not an age of voluntary self-discipline, and one misses in this joint enterprise the lack of a restraining and directing hand. However, this is an experiment from which all the participants, as well as the public, will carry away much that will give them a better perspective and appreciation of the aims and problems of sculpture.

A further search for sculpture in other parts of the island will bring still further and gratifying rewards. Over the west door of the Aviation Building the Spirit of Aviation (Taliabue) reveals the hand of the well-trained sculptor steeped in classical tradition. Robert Howard has contributed decorative vases and panels rich in movement and plastic values at the entrance to the Hall of Western States. The handsome redwood doors of the Shasta-Cascade Building (Carter) deserve special mention for their effective linear design, technically well adapted to the material in which they are carried out. There is, indeed, at Treasure Island a wealth of plastic decorative material, not always on the highway of the Exposition visitor, that merits attention, and a record of it will be found in the biographical appendix to this book.

Of the numerous decorative indoor sculptures, Robert Howard's playful Whales, supplemented by two decorative figures (Graham) astride of fishes, in the San Francisco Building, deserves special mention. This decorative fountain group done in synthetic black stone maintains standards of design and craftsmanship ordinarily not associated with exposition sculpture. It is to be hoped that this effective work will later find a permanent place in some appropriate setting more adequate to its monumental scale.

Chapter IV

LANDSCAPING, HORTICULTURE

THOUGH THE CREATING of a synthetic island was itself an impressive engineering feat, the seemingly magical transformation of this man-made island into a great walled city quickly excited curiosity, even delight, as the spacious buildings assumed shape and suggested meaning. Purely in terms of architecture, however, a city, no matter how effectively designed, is likely to be cold if lacking in the peculiar appeal that results from the integration of nature into an architectural aggregate. The task of producing this result is the special province of the landscape artist or designer. Unfortunately, in the popular mind this important profession suffers from a lack of clearly understood terms in which one may speak of its scope and responsibilities. Gardens at one time meant pleasure grounds of every kind, and "gardener" then had an adequate artistic sound—the designer of Kubla Khan's garden must have been an artist indeed; but as the meaning of the term "garden" gradually became specialized, the term "gardener" came to denote a mere grower of plants.

"Landscape gardener" was a title used by the artists of the eighteenth century to indicate a new tendency of that time, the search for "natural" as opposed to "formal" beauty. But as the landscape gardener lost sight of his artistic responsibilities, this term was replaced by the term "landscape architect," to suggest, no doubt, the close coöperation of two correlated arts and their common interest in design. However, the derivative term "landscape architecture" is not very satisfactory; nor, on the other hand, is "landscape artist," because it, also, suggests the peculiar province of the landscape painter, although "landscape art" is a good general term.

63

The profession by this time has generally adopted for its members the terms "landscape architect" and "landscape architecture." At the present Exposition the art of the horticulturist as such appears to make the main contribution, rather than that of the landscape architect, because of the fairly rigid prescriptions formulated by the architect himself. Therefore in this book, in order to avoid repetition, we shall use the term "landscape designer."

The values created by the landscape designer, Nature herself offers in great abundance, but often only too remote from cramped and oppressing conditions created by man's own hand, such as exist in so many of our cities. With the growth of cities and the gradual reduction of natural areas, landscape design has become increasingly an important profession, not only in supplementing the work of the architect, but also in giving the city dweller ready access to indispensable values of nature. The landscape designer may feel well repaid by the knowledge that thousands of people through the medium of his art approach not only a means of artistic enjoyment, but also a source of refreshment and recreation that are needed as a balance to the destructive and exhausting agencies of city existence.

The architect, the designer of buildings, deals with definite, often rigid, forms and balanced masses; the landscape designer uses vegetation, multiple and intricate in form, subject to the laws of growth and change. However, the landscape designer is not only concerned with the re-creating or preserving of natural values in man's environment; he must also produce aesthetically pleasing effects, and in that sense has another responsibility not unlike that of the architect himself.

At Treasure Island, through the medium of several enclosed and sheltered courts, the architect has opened to the landscape designer such opportunities as are rarely offered in any city. Because of the formal character of the Exposition plan, the landscape designer, like the sculptor, had to take his cue from the architect. The primary problem was not, therefore, the re-creating of a purely naturalistic garden spot aiming at an illusion of God-made nature, but rather the decorative enhancement of the framing of the buildings and the sculpture in

COURT OF THE CALIFORNIA BUILDING

PACIFIC HOUSE AS SEEN ACROSS THE LAGOON

terms of the vocabulary of the horticulturist, the supplementing of the comparatively rigid architectural forms by the much more flexible idiom of his own art.

It must be appreciated, however, that while on the one hand the landscape designer may provide a setting for architecture, he may at the other extreme, even at Treasure Island, occasionally create at least a suggestion of a woodland solitude, an effect of pure nature produced by age-long growth. The landscape designer, then, if he is to create a setting for a palace, must have not only an appreciation of the laws of design but also a knowledge of plant materials and of the natural effects that can be obtained by them. He must also have an understanding of the processes of nature, and a sensitiveness to the natural beauty of rock, wood, and water—elements that do not form the professional equipment of any other artist, unless it be the landscape painter. And it should be noted, further, that whereas the plastic arts of painting and sculpture translate nature into another medium, the landscape designer actually rivals Nature in her own terms. Yet, while he may compete with her, she herself works with him without depriving him of that chance for self-expression which every artist craves.

The landscape designer, then, in spite of his close subordination to architecture and his dependence upon nature, is not merely a skillful artisan or an obedient imitator of nature. When his title seems most appropriate, it implies the exercise of choice and inventiveness, the revelation of a personality. The public, therefore, in contemplating his work at the Exposition, should not merely yield to an instinctive inherent admiration for the charm of a natural world, but should become conscious that this is not only, in the strict sense, a love for natural things as such, but also a love for things that are beautiful, and unfamiliar and therefore striking, which are here expressed in a man-made garden. To a Californian the great variety of plants may not be impressive, but to many others this must be one of the most striking features of the Exposition.

Although theoretically there is no spot on earth that an artist could not beautify, in California we are generally not unmindful of the fact that a salubrious climate and an ample supply of water have made possible the creating of beautiful parks and gardens, public and private pleasure areas, in an amazingly short time. We take just pride in the genius and perseverance of John McLaren, who under these conditions brought into being in Golden Gate Park a horticultural perfection rarely achieved so quickly in regions climatically less favored than California. His industry, technical skill, and daring have set the pace for the younger generation that has created the charming garden effects on Treasure Island; and though perhaps the effects are not a permanent monument, they are at least a fitting tribute to the genial wizard of Golden Gate Park.

In spite of the oft-proclaimed advantages inherent in a California climate, Treasure Island presented no ordinary problem. Fixed time limits and unusual local conditions were handicaps that had to be overcome. The thousands of tons of silt lifted from the bottom of the Bay to create an island were not, apart from producing a "terra firma," a suitable basis for the consummation of a garden project. The saline constituents of the Bay silt admittedly are not favorable to the existence of plant material; in fact, pessimists early predicted wholesale failure for any attempt to make herbage grow at Treasure Island. Yet here we have a series of courts, open areas, and avenues bordered by luxuriant green lawns and trees enjoying their new environment.

To a scientist this is of course not an astonishing phenomenon. To an Exposition visitor, scientific theories of the chemistry of soils and the problems of plant nutrition may not be altogether welcome reading; yet something must be said. The unfavorable soil conditions were partly remedied at first by a fortunately copious rainfall in the winter of 1937–38 which washed out or greatly reduced the salt content of the earth. This content was then further reduced to a minimum by the addition of calcium sulphate. To the planting areas intended for plants requiring acid conditions, ammonium sulphate and aluminum sulphate were added. In anticipation of the horticultural requirements, thousands of trees and shrubs were grown in boxes and metal containers in the San Francisco nurseries at Balboa Park, and also at Berkeley

68

Neuhaus photo

PACIFIC HOUSE, DETAIL

and Saratoga. Many tons of humus were brought over to the island, and wherever planting was to be established a thick layer of ideal garden soil was spread over the porous sandy subsoil. Sunlight, water, skill, and care have done the rest, and the luxuriant foliage and new seasonal growth everywhere bear evidence of the efficiency of the Bureau of Horticulture of the Exposition (Girod).

The experience of creating the exposition of 1915 here gave an incalculable advantage. When, in May, 1938, barges first brought to the island the palms and olive trees which form the most widely used and effective tree material, it soon became apparent even to the skeptics that Treasure Island was not to be lacking in verdure, and when the Exposition opened, in February, 1939, the horticultural effects of the island were conspicuous alike for their decorative values and their healthy appearance.

However, another minor problem, not unlike the one met so successfully by McLaren in the initial steps of the development of Golden Gate Park, was that of counteracting the effect of the prevailing westerly wind blowing in through the Golden Gate, particularly during the summer months. Within the Exposition walls, the architecture itself affords the shelter and protection necessary for the normal existence of trees, plants, and flowers. The extensive exposed area on the west side presented a problem that was solved by the use of large numbers of various palms and other wind-resisting plant materials.

A palm thrives even in the most persistent salt breeze, and its normally fairly symmetrical shape, in yielding to the pressure of the sea breezes, becomes diverted into elegantly swaying forms. The tall palms* by the Exposition's western shore are placed informally, giving an effect of natural growth. Some of them are old specimens fifty feet high, and their acutely shaped shadows create, of an afternoon, interesting and lively patterns against the long, plain, outside horizontal walls of the Exposition city, breaking them up into interestingly related areas. In an enclosed area near the ferry entrance a veritable

---

* In Appendix III will be found a complete alphabetical list of all major and minor plant material used at the Exposition, the correct botanical name and the name of the country of origin being given for each plant.

grove of mature Canary Island palms has been set out, quite accidental in pattern and giving the effect of a sheltered oasis that has long been settled there.

At the base of the buildings other wind-resistant shrubs thrive, notably leptosperms and bamboo. They form a rich thicket of green, increasing in volume as they approach the corners where the elephant gates project upon the Marina. Other plant material that adds a note of variety in this region includes a few eucalypti with their graceful foliage, the exotic dracaena, broad-leaved New Zealand flax, and feathery pampas grass, and the very effective red-hot poker plant. The total effect is not particularly intimate, nor luxuriant, but rather utilitarian, adapting itself to the local conditions formulated by nature.

The great level area between water and buildings, called the Marina, has been set out with a variety of mesembryanthemums,* which yield a rich effect, mostly of warm colors. Here, a harmonious juxtaposition of tints—light pink, yellow, dark pink, orange, red, and scarlet—has formed a rich carpet, gay and stimulating to the eye, and giving an effect not unlike the suggestive and accidental pattern of an Oriental rug. As the Magic Carpet, this horticultural *tour de force* has received a great deal of public acclaim.

Passing from the Marina through the west gate and its adjoining forecourt, one enters the great central court. The landscaping here presents several unusual and artistically effective elements, particularly in the native madroño trees grouped near the base of the Tower of the Sun and at the entrance to the Court of the Moon and Stars. Madroños of this size, with a spread of more than twenty feet, are not often seen in private gardens, and to observe them in the temporary setting of an exposition is, to say the least, surprising. These sensitive wildwood trees were successfully moved from their forest habitat in San Mateo County and do not seem at all the worse for the experience. Their orange- and cinnamon-colored trunks and dark glossy foliage contribute an air of splendor and dignity.

Also native to North America, great specimens of magnolia are an-

* There is no popular substitute for this formidable name, unless it is ice plant.

JOHORE STATE PAVILION

73

other striking feature here; their glossy foliage, dark green above and a rusty orange underneath, is a marked decorative addition to the general horticultural color scheme of this court, which is keyed upon gold and bronze, modified, as are all horticultural palettes, by an abundance of greens.

Under the shelter of the magnolias and against the walls of the belvederes, many examples of the gold-dust tree may be seen. Cherry laurel is also used, beneath the balustrades of the four loggias, and adds its rich foliage to the sum total of the planting. Box in neatly trimmed hedges performs its architectural function in articulating areas given over to annuals. The major planting here is completed by two concentric rings of Valencia oranges laden with golden fruit; these were successfully transported to the Exposition from southern California (Montebello). Deciduous azaleas of several types in great numbers, in their typical range from yellow to orange and salmon-red, accentuate the color scheme, which is reflected also in the golden yellow of broom and the border plantings.

When the Exposition opened, this court was gay with yellow and white tulips, daffodils, blue hyacinths, and Lord Beaconsfield pansies. In the early summer and fall these were to be replaced by tuberous begonias, golden-bronze dahlias, and colorful pepper plants. The general aesthetic character of this court is of a simple, noble dignity, rather than of varied playfulness.

An entirely different mood is expressed in the Court of the Moon and Stars. This court holds many specimens of the eucalyptus, which are in keeping with its graceful architectural character. These stand in masses against the walls, and their feathery, open foliage determines the key to the general horticultural planting, which is light, sportive, and free. In front of the eucalypti, the fragrant California lilac has been freely used to add in early summer its atmospheric blue to the dominantly blue color of this court. Blackwood acacias, cherry laurel, pittosporums, California bay, Atlas cedar, and Monterey pine are also employed, to give that feeling of luxuriance which can only be accomplished by mass planting.

More madroño trees, as a sort of overflow from the adjoining central court, reach into this area. In the borders are massed many flowers and shrubs; among others, flowering quince, the glory bush, and summer lilac, yielding blue and purple flowers. Cobalt-blue veronica forms a trim, low hedge all around the lawn areas of this essentially pretty garden area. Rhododendrons, rose-pink and white, add both luxuriant foliage and bloom.

The Enchanted Garden, in front of the Yerba Buena Clubhouse, richly deserves its name. It is a sunken garden developed on three levels, the highest a little above the general level of the Exposition area, and thus it acquires an unusual plastic, three-dimensional quality. Each level is outlined by a hedge of boxwood. At the opening of the Exposition the beds enclosed by the boxwood were filled with blue pansies. These were to be succeeded by tulips of a rich pink.

The four corners of this garden each gain emphasis by the presence of five umbrageous Coast live oaks. Beneath these sturdy oaks pink rhododendrons have been massed. At the several approaches are stately dark green English yews, always effective in an architectural sense. Acacia, deodar cedar, Monterey pine, California privet, and other trees and shrubs add diversity of pattern and volume of foliage. This area not only has great formal dignity, but also reveals an unusual horticultural luxuriance. It is more truly a landscape design independent of an architectural frame: it is not so much a court formed by buildings as an independent garden area which gave to Mr. Girod, the supervising horticulturist, the one opportunity to create independently a work in his own medium. The fountain in the center and the stairs leading into it are, of course, architectural elements, but this time they are subsidiary to the horticultural effect.

Although we are tempted to linger here amid lavish planting effects, we must now retrace our steps to the Court of Reflections. Apart from the liberal use of the inevitable but effective green common to most trees and shrubs, red-leaved Japanese plums have been effectively used here as a color accent against the pink walls. Poplar and privet add in creating a solid mass of opulent greenery. Red-flowering eucalypti

76

YERBA BUENA CLUBHOUSE

are copiously used, as specimens bordering the pool or adding their characteristic foliage to the general planting. The border material in the terraces consists of early-blooming red rhododendrons, purple barberry, albelias, nandina, cydonia, and cotoneaster, all supplying, when in bloom or fruit, a red color element.

Since the general scheme is based on a lovely pink, derivations of red were also used in many ways in the minor planting. Red ranunculus, ruby violas, and tango-red pansies are here displayed in effective fashion. In May and June, red verbenas will be at their height, to be followed by brilliant red salvia. Later, from July until early fall, red amaryllis, red begonias, red phlox, and red salvia will be the main attraction and will continue to emphasize the color peculiar to this court.

The adjoining square court, the Court of Flowers, boldly lives up to its reputation for gaiety and variety. Its color progression is conceived as contrast in variety, rather than harmony. Three varieties of eucalyptus are used in the corners of the court, their shadows casting animated patterns; and tall Italian poplars stand at the base of the arch, accentuating its aspiring forms. In the corners, mature specimens of tree ferns give an exotic and precious quality to the planting, their majestic, curving fronds reaching the round arches of the ambulatory. At the base of the walls and terraces a great variety of shrubs tempt the eye—the rockrose, heath, fuchsia, and eugenia with their glossy foliage, white-flowered choisya, and others too numerous to mention.

North of the central court, the Court of the Seven Seas reveals an impressive display of many specimens of eucalyptus from thirty to fifty feet in height. Whatever we may argue against this Australian visitor, now so well established in California, as a tree against or in combination with architecture it has few rivals for picturesqueness and decorative effectiveness. Pittosporum, poplar, acacia, and laurel here also supply most of the major planting, while smaller trees and shrubs, including the flowering peach, the broom, the myrtle, and the snowball bush add variety to the areas in front of the taller trees. The yellow-and-white horticultural color scheme of this court is maintained, moreover, by violas, daisies, tulips, and many other annuals.

The Court of Pacifica uses planting as an accent to architecture rather than for the development of a garden. Here, great free-standing fifty-five-foot specimens of eucalyptus flank the statue of Pacifica. Along the perimeter of the court stand more than twenty large specimens of loquat, creating striking dark accents against the plain walls of the enclosing architecture. Incense cedars rise gravely below the Bruton mural, and Japanese privet, Victorian box, and cherry laurel contribute to the mass planting. The central fountain is handsomely enriched by many prostrate junipers, which play in well with the architecture. Blue, white, and pink hyacinths, orange and blue violas, yellow marguerites, and wallflowers help to carry the blue-and-gold color accents through the season.

The planting on the eastern part of Treasure Island largely repeats the horticultural vocabulary of the courts. In the Central American group, aloes create amongst other typical plants an individual note. Within the county group are concealed several garden units created under the supervision of Mr. Daniels, Mr. Shepherd, and others; in them, planting material has been displayed not only for its artistic effectiveness, but also for its unusualness and rarity.

Even the Californian, accustomed to the richness, variety, and consecutive effect of gardens, is likely not to remain unaffected by what has been accomplished at the Exposition, and to the outsider Treasure Island must be a wonderland of the gardener's art, the significance of which can only be appreciated if one imagines the Exposition devoid of horticultural elements. It is not unlikely that many an Exposition visitor will regard this horticultural display as the Exposition's preeminent and charming element, refreshing and joyous.

Grau photo

TOWER OF THE CHINESE VILLAGE

81

Chapter V

THE COLOR EFFECTS

THAT COLOR ENLIVENS everything it touches is an accepted axiom. An unconscious exclusion of color from our man-made surroundings indicates a lack of appreciation of the special aesthetic pleasures which color alone is capable of giving; its deliberate denial is nothing less than the negation of life. Rightly we speak of color in a broad sense as the epitome of living.

We normally and readily yield to the charm of color in nature; its wide and conscious use today in our utilitarian surroundings, and no less in works of art, is convincing proof of its wide appeal. In an artistic inventory of the twentieth century, not only form but also color reveals significantly, in spite of the apparent chaos of our time, inherent vigor and a spirit of adventure that will aid us in conquering the perplexities of human society.

Colors may express all sorts of qualities: they may be clear or hazy, warm or cold, light or dark, dull or bright; and symbolically these qualities may be translated so variously that they may be described by an infinite number of adjectives. Thus, color may affect us as shallow, crude, brutal, sweet, garish, sensuous, loud, pretentious, and so on, depending upon an individual's associative experiences in life.

Colors may readily be modified by the addition of white or black. When white is added, a tint is the result; the addition of black produces a shade. Almost all the colors used at Treasure Island are tints, because the addition of a moderate amount of white gives to a color a sense of lightness, of airiness, of cheer—a joyous quality in keeping with the professed festal mood of an exposition. Shades have a substantial and dignified quality, but are also heavy; furthermore, they produce psychologically the opposite effect of tints. Unless they occasionally appear as accents, shades are not a conspicuous part of the Exposition color scheme.

An exposition in our age without the stimulus of color is unthinkable, because color, as we should again be reminded, has become in the twentieth century such an important factor not only in the pictorial but also in the decorative arts that we regard it as indispensable to life and living. Expositions have not always been remarkable for color; in fact, the Chicago exposition of 1893 widely advertised itself as the "White City," without realizing that white, like black, is a negation of color.* Of course, white suggests hygienic and moral associations, and it may be that in 1893 at Chicago white suggested a connotation desirable in the western metropolis of that day. White was also largely the general effect at Buffalo in 1901, and again at St. Louis in 1904. It was at San Francisco in 1914 that its spell as a dominant exposition color was first broken in the United States.

In fact, the exposition of 1915 at San Francisco left a special heritage in having at least suggested the wider use of color in a drab urban environment. Jules Guérin, the director of color of that memorable enterprise, while he refrained from striking contrasts, succeeded at least in steeping the entire exposition in a warm harmony that was effective in its soothing tonal agreeableness. George Sterling's "cool gray city of love" then awoke to the realization that its inner emotions might become revealed more appropriately in the chromatic terms of the exposition. During the years that followed, Guérin's insinuating demonstration of color was not forgotten in California. But it was not color as such, but rather the warm general tone of the popular imitation travertine, that gave rise to pleasurable sensations; Guérin's color was essentially a heightening of qualities inherent in the material.

Since that time, color at expositions has been experimented with at various fairs in different and new ways. Chicago in 1933 not only went into extravagant experiments in pure and functional form, but also in its use of color it defied the traditional laws of color usage. Rather ex-

* Oswald called black and white the colorless colors, *unbunte Farben,* as compared to the *bunte Farben* such as orange, red, blue, green.

84

DETAIL OF COURTYARD, PAVILION OF FRENCH INDO-CHINA

perimentally than conclusively, almost pure spectral color was applied to scattered architectural units. Although exciting enough, they remained to the eye mostly paint rather than color. New York this year has organized its color effect on the spectral system, radiating from center toward periphery.

Before paint can function as color it must inevitably be referred to some artistic principle. A box full of paints may indeed be gay, but one misses in looking at it the intelligent application of organization, modification, studied contrast, sympathetic analogy—in short, some recognizable order. Exciting as any strong hue may be for the moment, it is doubtful whether it will hold one's attention for even so short a time as is allotted to expositions. By now, expositions everywhere have abandoned white as a satisfactory color, if it can be called a color; and if they have not worked with a palette of many hues, they have at least shown a more sympathetic general tone, as in the tawny yellow of the Dallas fair in 1936. In order to deal successfully with so important a department of art, the Golden Gate International Exposition intrusted itself to the guiding hand of a director of color (Stanton), who worked out an appropriate and varied chart.

At the Panama-Pacific International Exposition of 1915, four color tones appeared on the warm surface of the travertine stucco: a warm red resembling orange, and a cool red approaching pink; a cold blue bordering on purple, and another, warmer, blue containing an element of green. These four colors, and no others, were used wherever an opportunity presented itself, but the total effect of the exposition was, in spite of these local accents, one of a rich, appealing tonal harmony.

If the color philosophies of expositions of recent dates in America may be used to elucidate the color of the Golden Gate International Exposition, it may be done as follows. In 1915, in San Francisco, color was used harmoniously as a mellow, soothing, tonal entity. In Chicago, in 1933, color was chiefly employed as a powerful chromatic stimulant; almost no traditional harmonies were attempted; individual color effects were not only daring in their intensity, but also in their oppositional combination of hues.

87

At the present fair, the color scheme is a happy combination of the two types just described. The palette comprises eighteen separate color expressions, mostly tints, and gold. The foundation to which the tints are applied is a stucco base of a sympathetic warm tone called Exposition Ivory; by comparison, a little lighter and cooler than the travertine of 1915. Into its surface has been pressed a substance called "Zonolite," a commercial product which is the result of a process of heating mica to a high temperature so that it is broken up into flakes and separate small leaves, resembling luminous gold. Pressed into the wet plaster, it contributes to the surface a living quality such as is normally found in quarried stone, and it is permanent and lasting in effect. The surface of the stucco shows many small irregularities and openings that reveal little particles of the glittering mica, and this gives variety and a rich textural quality not to be found in a polished smooth surface.

The Exposition palette is endowed for the occasion with alluring suggestive names. There is a bright luminous light yellow tint that is called poetically Sun-of-Dawn Yellow, a darker richer yellow (Pagoda Yellow), a rather neutral yellow (Old Mission Fawn), and a still darker yellow curiously called Polynesian Brown (in reality, it is a tint of yellow orange). There are also four greens: a very pale bluish green tint (Evening Star Blue), a rich warm yellow green (Hawaiian Emerald Green), and a cooler green similar in tone values, called Ming Jade Green, which is used in both a lighter and a darker tone. The reds are similarly graded from a light (Pebble Beach) coral to a warm orange (Santa Clara Apricot) to a darker brick red (Imperial Dragon Red). There are also four blues: a light gray purple blue (Pacific Blue), a very luminous green blue (Del Monte Blue), a deeper blue (China Clipper Blue), and a blue to which a little black has been added (Southern Cross Blue).

Three rather neutral colors complete the palette: a so-called écru, a taupe (Santa Barbara Rose), and a mauve (Death Valley). Gold has also been employed wherever it seemed called for, particularly in enhancing the plastic effectiveness of some of the sculpture, as for instance the great panels between the Towers of the East.

GATEWAY TO THE COURT OF SPAIN

The fanciful appelations given by the Director of Color to these hues are obviously created for this special occasion, and the Exposition visitor will do best to enjoy them as he happens to find them, without benefit of nomenclature. It must be remembered that seasonal color names are the result of a natural craving for change, and, like fashions generally, are soon replaced by other color designations based on momentary associations. The only dependable way is to describe colors in terms of the spectrum: as yellow, red, blue, orange, green, violet. Their artistic use is dependent upon definite methods of modification, such as the addition of white or black, or their association as analogues, or in terms of contrasting complementaries either separately or in combinations of the diverse methods in an infinite number of ways.

It might not be out of place to explain briefly at this point the three more commonly used methods of artistically effective color modifications or selections. A monochromatic color scheme is simply an arrangement of different tints or shades—or both—of one color, such as is commonly observed in the green of foliage or in the utilitarian light brown, brown, and one or two darker browns. A complementary color scheme is based upon the principle of opposition of two colors from the spectral ring, such as orange-red and blue-green, or yellow and violet; such contrasting combinations are striking and effective and are common both in nature and in art. By far the most pleasing and suggestive color combinations are analogues of similar colors, such as yellow, yellow-orange, orange, and red-orange, or blue, blue-violet, violet, and red-violet.*

Colors of great intensity are normally not enjoyable in large areas; they more commonly serve the purpose of accents. At Treasure Island two intensive blue colors, a light blue-green (Del Monte Blue) and a darker, equally intense blue (China Clipper Blue) are to be found on relatively small areas on doors and entrances. Gold, because of its great power and, no doubt, its cost, also serves as an accent, as in the gilded Phoenix atop the Tower of the Sun or on the reliefs between the Temples of the East.

---

* The Exposition visitor who wishes to pursue this subject further may consult the author's *World of Art*.

In general it will be observed that the colors of lesser intensity, the lighter tints, are applied over the largest areas, such as architectural panels, to differentiate the several courts. Almost every court has been worked out in terms of a definite color scheme, mostly of analogous color complemented by the colors of nature. Stronger color accents have been created on doors, entrances, vestibules of towers and palaces, lighting fixtures and bunting, and here and there on sculpture.

The main entrances of the enclosing walls have been emphasized by vertical color bands. The relatively small doors carry an intense green, marking at a glance their focal function. Above them a light yellow panel reaches to the eaves of the building, and on either side of this glowing tint, narrow yellow-green vertical bands make an accent. On either side are vertical, larger, well-proportioned masses of a luminous pink (Pebble Beach Coral) framed by a stronger red (Santa Clara Apricot), completing a color scheme at once happy and architecturally effective in its masses.

To discuss briefly the chromatic treatment of the various courts, it seems logical to begin with the central court, the Court of Honor. Color here is supplied suggestively by the color of the stucco, the horticultural elements, and those of nature generally. The lighting standards are the one consciously used color accent. Since this court is a kind of official reception room for the many and diverse emissaries to the Exposition from all over the world, it must in the nature of things be dignified, even noncommittal. Relying a good deal upon architectural effectiveness, it is exceptional in its restraint. Very large silk American flags, recalling in their size and placement the great banners of St. Mark's Square, are the dominant and logical decoration of this great court, supplying the requisite flavor of hospitality.

Moreover, a unique colorful accent here is the music provided by the forty-three bells which are installed in the tower. Their varied sounds are analogous to the colors displayed in distant areas, and it is not unlikely that here a combination of form, color, and sound would prove too much for the aesthetic receptivity of the ordinary human being. A super-art which will appeal satisfactorily and simultaneously

MISSION TRAILS BUILDING

to all the senses has long been in the minds of aesthetic adventurers, but it will probably defeat itself because the limitation of human psychology and physiology is the one reason, apart from the technical problems, for the separate existence of the different arts. There is a natural limit which the aesthetic experimenter must recognize, unless he is satisfied with a temporary sensational success.

To the south, in the Court of the Moon and Stars, a light green-blue, called Evening Star Blue, has been used to recall in the daytime the special color appeal of this court at night. All the tints here are derivatives of blue and green, all clear and somewhat evanescent, sentimental but quite suited to the deliberate program of the designer to recall here the court of the caliphs in the *Arabian Nights*.

In the Court of Reflections the pervading color is a light coral red (Pebble Beach Coral), reflected and reëchoed in the planting and again accentuated by it. Compared with the sentimental mood of the Court of the Moon and Stars, this court reflects only a cheery, idyllic quality. No literary ideas are invoked here. Of all the courts it has the most straightforward quality, a result no doubt of a conviction that architecture at its best gives satisfactory aesthetic results without literary and sentimental concomitants. The many delightful color pictures created by the surface of the pool are a further claim to distinction. Particularly from the eastern and western ends, entrancing pictures are revealed in these placid waters.

From here we pass through the Arch of the Winds into the Court of Flowers, where a deep apricot red speaks sympathetically from the walls in the surrounding ambulatory. The pagan and sylvan atmosphere of this court is greatly enhanced by the use of many different colors supplied by foliage and by blooms harmonized by the foliage pattern. Variety of form and color is the emphasis, and sound plays no small part in it. Water here, in contrast to that in the Court of Reflections, is never still; it adds its stimulating sound to the atmosphere of joyousness and exuberance. The luxuriance of form and color and sound suggest the even greater splendor near by, in the towers which terminate the Exposition palaces in the east.

The Towers of the East, recalling the pagodas of Rangoon, are treated chromatically with such extravagance that hardly any of the stucco color is left to assert itself. No doubt in order to achieve the traditional splendor and sense of opulence of the Orient, color is here employed in its emotionally most effective terms. It is debatable, however, how far color can go in enriching architectural forms, and one has some justifiable misgivings in discovering that the pattern of masonry on the bulging walls of the towers is produced with the aid of the painter's brush. Athough this is "exposition architecture," deception carried to such a degree is likely to result in a disappointment to the close observer. In this neighborhood, color combined with gold has been employed extravagantly, the latter left in its pure state or tempered to suggest the patina of age. Most of the colors are chromatically of greater strength than those in the other parts of the Exposition, resolving themselves into mysterious and exotic harmonies.

To complete our investigations, we now return to the Court of Honor and pass from it into the Court of the Seven Seas, a majestic *via triumphalis,* its perspective heightened by many great flag standards designed as bases of ship prows from which rise masts and spars carrying banners a little weak in color which move on the gentle breezes. The base of this court carries neutral colors derived from buffs and reds. Color here is not so much created in terms of pigments as in the general spirit of adventure which animates the court.

Finally, we once more enter the Court of Pacifica, with its intensified architectural scale. Color here functions as separate accents such as are produced from the sixteen tubular lighting standards, and produces emotionally effective values. Color in the sense of life or vitality triumphs here in many ways—in the restless exuberance of the fountain sculpture, in the strong contrasting note of the mysterious and static Pacifica, and in the mural on the west side, which in a sense is the color spectacle of this impressive court, and which paves the way for a discussion of a significant part of the color scheme, the mural decorations.

THE PHOENIX CROWNING THE TOWER OF THE SUN

97

Chapter VI

THE MURAL DECORATIONS

EVEN A CASUAL STROLL through Treasure Island should convince the visitor to the Exposition that the summation of its chromatic expression is the mural paintings effectively distributed in the architectural ensemble. These special accents not only offer to a heightened degree color as such, but with this visually stimulating element they combine an additional attraction of conveying ideas, of telling stories—an inseparable element of representational painting. Furthermore, compared to color used as a two-dimensional embellishment of architecture in terms of large, flat-color areas, a mural painting reflects the individuality of the artist in a heightened plastic interpretation of color and form, and this results inevitably in a greater emotional appeal. The Architectural Commission, as well as the several individual architects personally, is responsible for the artistic success of the Fair, and is to be congratulated upon its conviction that California's painters could be relied upon to meet adequately their assigned task in this field. It is in this department that its confidence seems particularly well justified.

Although inevitably some of the decorations are more successful as murals in the best sense, others perhaps function as enlarged illustrations emphasizing the subject-matter or story, and only to a lesser degree the abstract, formal-element qualities requisite to artistic enjoyment. One of the primary requisites of a mural painting, that it must not destroy the two-dimensionality of the wall of which it is an integral part, is also not always conclusively demonstrated at Treasure Island. Yet, taking the murals in their totality, their outstanding merit in spite of certain occasional shortcomings is their native independence, avoidance of hackneyed ideas, and evidence of an intelligent eagerness on the part of the artist to experiment with new technical methods.

Mural painting in its heyday under Giotto's inspiration meant essentially fresco painting, but the use of this most appropriate medium eventually declined, to give way to all sorts of unhappy compromises. Fortunately, mural painting in recent times, particularly in the Far West, has again come to mean fresco painting, and also a variety of effective mosaic techniques peculiarly well adapted to the decoration, by means of pictorial ideas, of the walls of public and private buildings—that is to say, of permanent, durably constructed buildings, and not temporary "expositional" ones.

Expositions, unfortunately, are not composed of permanent buildings, no matter how convincingly they may simulate enduring materials; and besides their shortcomings resulting from this basic inadequacy, exposition buildings completed at the last moment leave no time for the execution of frescoes on their walls. For this reason mainly, fresco in its true sense was out of the question for Treasure Island, and the mural paintings, with several notable exceptions, as in 1915, had to be painted on canvas, or on "Masonite" and other similar material, to be affixed to the surfaces where they were to function as decorative accents. This procedure entails another obvious disadvantage. A large picture painted in a studio, or even in a large loft, away from its ultimate location, is necessarily subject to a preliminary estimate of its ultimate artistic effectiveness. However, the experienced artist usually has no serious misgivings over this problem, because he is fairly well able to calculate in advance the scale of his design, the effectiveness of his pattern, the requisite intensity of his colors, and other formal values that will determine the artistic success of his work. Since several of the murals at the Exposition were created under these handicaps, it is surprising that their shortcomings on this score are nearly negligible. Lack of time was the one really serious handicap, and it caused some lapses into inadequate drawing and color which prolonged consideration would have obviated.

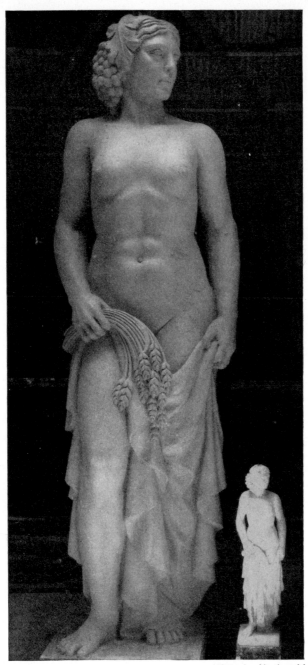

AGRICULTURE—TOWER OF THE SUN

Although their number is fairly large, the task of considering the murals critically is neither fatiguing nor time-consuming. This pleasant task may be carried out either as a separate enterprise or as part of a general Exposition tour.

In the Court of Honor, which confessedly relies upon its architectural values, neither color nor mural decorations are in evidence. Perhaps the architect felt that breadth of conception and nobility of architectural design would suffer from the intrusion of mural painting.

Not far away, the south towers of the Court of the Moon and Stars contain, somewhat inconspicuously placed, four vertical panels that may easily be overlooked. In the one to the east, two distinguished and experienced women muralists (Forbes, Puccinelli) have done good teamwork, each contributing two very striking wall paintings, the theme being "The First Garden." These refreshing panels are teeming with decoratively developed human, animal, and floral forms, which are carefully thought out without being in the least labored or set. Their color is varied and gay, and it functions clearly and freely without interference from disturbing naturalistic lights and shadows. Their linear design has depth without disturbing the function of the wall. These essentially decorative paintings are at once enjoyable and effective. They take us back to the days when the world was young and the primal wonder of man manifested itself in countless questing ways.

In the west tower, Poole and Bergman have each contributed two paintings similar in size to those just discussed. These decorations obviously are the work of two artists of very different ideals, and they are unfortunately not very companionable in their confined location. Poole's subject is early California at work and modern California at play; in one panel a miner washes out gold in one of Poole's typical coastal landscapes, and in another a family group around a campfire in a similar setting symbolizes play. Poole's capacity for decorative values has been demonstrated for years at our exhibitions, and here at the Exposition his decorative style again is easily recognizable. However, the mood of both his paintings is rather frigid. The color is lacking in joyousness; it is tonal rather than chromatic.

Bergman's two panels are allegorical of the thrilling days of early California history with their lure of gold and its epochal significance to men. On one side, a miner works feverishly to reach the hidden treasure, bits of it being tantalizingly dropped into his path by a figure overhead which symbolizes the precious metal. On the opposite side, a miner pays tribute to the figure of the Goddess of Fortune, who here is surrounded by characters typical of early California days. The story is clear, and, what is more significant, the purely abstract qualities of the artist's designs are abundantly developed throughout his composition. There are no uninteresting areas in his pictures. The color is rich and has a peculiarly agreeable and personal technical quality that gives his work a tapestrylike appearance.

On the inside of the great arch dividing the Court of Reflections from the Court of Flowers, Hugo Ballin is represented by two unusually narrow and high panels (ten feet wide by forty-five feet high). The situation of these panels inside of a relatively narrow arch makes an adequate study from inside the arch somewhat unsatisfactory. It is only when one views them from a distance and obliquely from one of the adjoining courts that one's eye is able to encompass the entire composition. The Winds in their varied qualities, like Malmquist's themes in the central tower, are symbolized by human beings. Their scale is in keeping with their monumental setting. All the figures, even those closest to the observer, are necessarily greater than life size, and those in the upper reaches of the design are drawn eighteen feet tall in order to counteract the loss in apparent dimensions. Mr. Ballin's academic draftsmanship is more than adequate to the task.

The compositions reveal a marked sense of movement, the result of a consistent use of a letter S line in the arrangement of the pictorial material. The effective disposition of the human forms surging upwards in rhythmical fashion imparts to this composition a certain dynamic sense. Both panels are enlivened, moreover, with a great variety of effectively distributed symbolic detail that not only lends interest to the surface of the painting but also amplifies the pictorial theme.

EVENING STAR—COURT OF THE MOON AND STARS

The color of these two canvases inclines a little toward sweetness, and the negative areas—those resulting from the placing of the figures against a light sky—are without that sense of substance which is necessary to the two-dimensional wall of which they are a part. In the main, however, these ambitious canvases sustain themselves in supplementing the uplifting quality of the very lofty arch in which they are placed.

In the arcade of the Court of Flowers, Millard Sheets has contributed six panels on lively and original themes. Originally, three of these were allotted to Frank van Sloun, but his unexpected and untimely death necessitated another arrangement, and Sheets became the logical successor. Sheets's technical expertness, his pictorial inventiveness, are too well known to require comment here. In these six panels he has given striking evidence of his mastery of a field in which he is not so widely known as he is in easel painting. Apart from an eclectic use of historic formulas in the composition, there is a marked sense of originality in all these dynamic designs. The general theme for the three panels on the north side is "California History." The first depicts the Spanish Era, symbolized by two great figures representing the conquistador and the padre. The second panel, the Gold Era, is depicted by a large miner characteristic of the period, symbolizing the desire for acquisition. The third panel, the central one, symbolizes California in modern times as a Land of the Sun to which the world is converging by sea and plane. California is depicted from the Pacific to the High Sierra, and overhead is an ancient Mayan face which is used as the sun symbol.

The themes of the pictures on the south side are "Daytime in Agriculture," "Clocktime in Industry," and "Infinite Time," which is depicted by a large figure of Destiny weaving the time fabric. These compositions seem the least hackneyed of any to be seen at Treasure Island. Although the artist's work compositionally draws upon the treasury of the past, it does not take one back to the cheap allegories of another day, but boldly takes hold of contemporary themes and translates them into vital decorations, alive and stimulating. The well-sustained sense of vitality in ideas, form, and color of these wall paintings well fits the general character of this court, its liveliness, its joyousness, its spontaneity.

In the Court of the Seven Seas, Armin Hansen and John T. Stoll share honors equally in the twelve paintings at the recessed entrances of the Exposition palaces which bound this area. Hansen's six panels all represent themes of the sea, more particularly ships, a subject with which he has long been familiar and in which he early established an enviable reputation both as easel painter and as etcher.

His paintings here are done in monochrome washes, dexterous and free in technique, well balanced in composition, and varied in design. Their effect, however, is rather that of an illustration than a mural decoration; and, placed as they are in self-contained enclosed areas, they are more enjoyable as easel pictures than as mural decorations in the special sense. Their technical legerdemain is most ingratiating. They show, too, an extraordinary economy of material; achieving solidity, nevertheless, by the simple process of using the substantial tone of the exposition stucco as a basic color. The absence of a varied chromatic treatment is compensated by variety of form and a spontaneous technical quality that is both refreshing and suggestive.

Mr. Stoll's six paintings do not so much deal with ships as with men who sail ships, and with episodes in their hazardous life which here have been depicted in a variety of ways and compositional solutions somewhat strained and ill at ease. His color scheme for these appropriate themes is almost monochromatic. Whatever slight color qualities Stoll has employed are almost lost in their outdoor setting. Their effect in these pictures is striking, but also a little hard and mannered in technique.

It is in the gigantic Court of Pacifica that we are confronted with an adventure in mural decoration, unusual and bold, both in its great size and in its technical novelty. It is the work of three sisters (Bruton) distinguished for artistic achievement in a variety of ways.

The colossal size of this mural (fifty-seven feet high by one hundred and fifty-seven feet long) marks it as one of the largest undertak-

RAIN—ENCHANTED GARDEN

109

ings of this type. But this is not its sole claim to distinction. It is of peculiar and special interest because it represents a technical innovation which has been made possible by modern industrial technical research. It is in fact both painting and sculpture at one and the same time, a polychromatic low relief carved out of modern material. The technique involves the use of several superimposed layers of wood-fiber insulation material of different thicknesses attached to four- by eight-foot sections of plywood board. The wood fiber used represents three separate thicknesses, ranging from one-half inch to two inches. The design was first created in strictly plastic terms resembling low relief by carving the forms out of the fiber boards. For the most plastic passages the use of three thicknesses of board was necessary; in the flatter areas, often only the thickness of one fiber board was required. In order to render the design intelligible and, in view of the colossal scale, to insure pictorial effectiveness, a simplified stylistic treatment was indicated, and this treatment, although the product of several collaborating artists, is consistently maintained throughout, insuring a sense of unity.

The subject of this impressive scheme is called "Peaceful Relations," that is to say, the harmonious social and cultural relations of the peoples living on the borders of the Pacific Ocean. The center of the design is dominated by the colossal figure of a forty-foot Buddha, representing Asia, at whose feet kneels the figure of a woman symbolic of the races. On either side of this central group and on a smaller scale are processions of people (towering twenty-four feet in height) moving toward the symbolic figure in the center. On the left are the natives and tribes of Asia; on the right, European peoples. The rest of the composition is filled with numerous decorative elements recalling the achievements of these different peoples in the arts and sciences.

The color scheme is restrained, but effective in clearly defining the different elements of the design. The colors are fairly warm, and range through ochres and terra-cotta tints to more brilliant reds. The processions are clearly defined in a very light ivory tint against a gold background, and the central figure of Buddha, by contrast with the kneeling figure, is presented in dark values. Some of the more abstract forms carry light blues and greens, the totality suggesting a polychromatic Renaissance panel. In contemplating this ambitious technical experiment, one wonders if perhaps a stronger chromatic treatment or perhaps the complete elimination of color might not have set off to better advantage its fine sculptural qualities.

On the side walls of the eastern approach in this court are two murals by an old and experienced hand in this field, Maynard Dixon. In the very nature of things his designs must take a secondary place, but they are no less effective in the special responsibility they assume. On one side is a decorative design, "Plowed Land"; on the opposite side, "Grass Land." Both designs have a charm that results from a clear and simple use of form and color. Dixon here refrains from any new adventures, and these decorations in their straightforwardness reflect qualities long recognized in his easel paintings. The color scale is consciously restricted to the warm earth hues characteristic of the palette of the fresco painter.

A further exploration of the Exposition area reveals several other noteworthy mural schemes, notably the gay and colorful decorative treatment of the façade of the Federal Building. Here, on a surface measuring sixty by one hundred and sixty feet, exceeding the Bruton mural in size, Herman Voltz and a staff of assistants have depicted the "Conquest of the West" by land and by water. A gallery of historic characters from pioneer days to modern times here passes in review. Men and women widely separated in time and endeavor, who made or are making history, are distinguishable: Kit Carson, intrepid mountaineer; Luther Burbank, skillful propagator of plants; Father Junípero Serra, saintly priest; Timothy Pflueger, bold protagonist of contemporary architecture, and many more. The design is carried out directly on the wooden base that constitutes the surface finish of this enormous exterior wall area. The organization of the pictorial material is not always effective, clear, or in complete harmony with the deliberately simplified formal concept of the architecture of the Federal Building. It is a far cry from the monochromatic panels of Hansen or

THE RAINBOW—RAINBOW FOUNTAIN

113

the academic color of Ballin or the rich tapestry of Bergmann to the pure jubilant color of this decoration, which both in scale and in chomatic power carry its message to a great distance clear across the lagoon. Such gaiety, though most enjoyable, is usually not associated with the idea of the government of a great country.

As a technical experiment these gigantic paintings will bear watching, since the permanent colors employed will have a chance to prove their worth in a California sunshine. The blue is the beautiful monastral blue of recent perfection, all the yellows and reds are cadmiums, the greens are mixtures of these colors, and the earths have been keyed up by cadmium yellow, oranges, and reds. The several grays of course need not give concern.

Flanking this colossal scheme, in a sense completing it, Lucien Labaudt has provided the designs for two similarly gigantic mural paintings executed directly on the outside walls of the California Building and the California Auditorium. Their themes are the industries and the arts of this state. Again the scale of the figures is several times life size and the effect is monumental and in keeping with both the man-made and the natural environment of the area. These heroic designs are well integrated into the wall, and this is to be remarked as one of their best qualities. Their coloring is warmer but also less gay than that of the murals on the Federal Building. However, the total effect is dignified, warm, and agreeable.

Not far away, Marian Simpson has contributed two large murals in the arcade of the inner court of the Alameda-Contra Costa Building. The basic color of these decorations is a rich and warm light terracotta tone and the linear design is carried out in analogies of darker colors of similar hues, contrasted by malachite green accents. Against this effective background, enlivened by a rhythmical design ingeniously derived from the geographic contours of the East Bay counties, semiabstract figures have been placed at well-calculated intervals. On one side these represent "Rural Life," and on the other "Urban Life." The total effect is both interesting and decorative and reflects the self-assurance of the experienced muralist.

In the main lobby of the San Francisco Building the walls above the balcony have been enlivened by a series of sprightly, somewhat casual decorations (Berlandina). These rhythmical embellishments symbolically glorify four of San Francisco's claims to distinction: its ballet, its cuisine, its opera, and its symphony. The free-and-easy manner in which they are carried out may be described as a brilliant *tour de force*. It is, however, somewhat lacking in the architectural qualities for which the environment seems to call.

Below the balcony, the "Industries of the Bay Area" have been depicted (Born). These carefully thought out and constructed designs encompass a great variety of subject-matter, each is clearly and vividly set forth, and at the same time each reveals a wealth of enjoyable abstract qualities of form and color. These murals are obviously the work of a well-disciplined draftsman blessed with a rich sense of color. It is fortunate that they occupy the position below the balcony, because their architectural quality, their well-maintained two-dimensional surface quality, helps to sustain the wall which supports the balcony above.

On the eastern side of this building complex—that is to say, in the ballroom of the California Building—a large mural (Del Pino) fills the wall containing the stage. The theme, "A Spanish Fiesta," seems appropriate in every way to a room devoted to recreation and merry-making. The artist, himself a Spaniard by birth, has drawn upon the store of picturesque customs and traditions of his native country, so rich in color, gallantry, and romance. He has translated these into a design exuberant in form and has steeped them in a glowing, somewhat theatrical, but emotionally effective coloring. Caballeros, dancers, señoras playing guitars and señoritas in gorgeous shawls and laces have supplied the material for a grand fantasia of color and form. Of all the settings for a mural, this ballroom with its overpowering red color scheme offered a difficult problem. The artist has met it as well as could be expected.

The same artist is represented at the Exposition by another mural painting—on the outside walls of one of the buildings that constitute

SPIRIT OF AERIAL TRANSPORTATION—AVIATION HANGAR

117

the Temple of Religion group. In subject, color, and treatment it is the direct antithesis of the "Spanish Fiesta." The theme is "The Hand of God," and the work is a symbolic frieze presenting man's course on earth as directed by a divine power. Here man is progressively depicted from infancy to maturity, engaged in play and in work, engrossed in love, in his family, and finally in his physical decline and death. The guiding hands of the Creator are seen at the beginning, the middle, and the end of this extensive painting, ushering him into this world, blessing his efforts, and receiving him at the end of his earthly career.

It takes an artist of sound academic discipline to deal simultaneously with two so divergent themes, but in spite of this and the handicap of time, Mr. Del Pino has succeeded well. In the "Spanish Fiesta" the technique is free, unrestricted, joyous, impressionistic, the color gay and emotionally appealing to heighten the idea of the theme. In "The Hand of God" a sober fresco technique, linear, restrained, and dignified, is employed, and the color is restricted to the simple range of earth colors of the fresco painter and the total effect is compatible with the setting and the story.

In Pacific House, several decorations in different and novel media add a singularly effective and enjoyable note to an artistic structure. Here, Miguel Covarrubias has created six large decorative and illustrated maps of the countries adjacent to the Pacific Ocean. Their peoples, their fauna and flora, economy, art and culture, means of housing, and transportation, all have been woven into a modern tapestry of joyful color and form, sharp and precise in concept. Without being dramatic, the total effect is gay, even exhilarating, full of interesting information that is often quaintly humorous. There is not an idle moment in any of them.

In this joyous, artistic, and instructive atmosphere a colored leaded glass map (Taylor) illustrating the modern trade routes of the Pacific will be found on the north balcony. It is artificially illuminated from behind, and apart from the information it conveys it possesses fine qualities of design and an appeal possessed only by the medium in which it is executed.

119

Here also, and on the south balcony, other decorative maps (Hiler) have been installed, emphasizing again both information and artistic enjoyment. The enormous plastic glazed terra-cotta map (Sotomayor) of the Pacific area, situated in the center of the main floor, is technically unique, and its varied, fascinating blues, as seen through the water, which carries part of the design, create a picture of great charm.

Aside from the murals singled out for discussion in the preceding pages, the Exposition, particularly the palaces, presents many evidences that the creative artist has "gone democratic" in serving commerce and trade. It is not the traditional commercial art which here repeats its trite and too obviously clever ideas, but the type of freely creative artistic expression that serves, for example, as a background for the display of the California Packing Corporation in the Food Palace (Knowles). Here the various food products of land and sea have been set forth on a light ground in a sprightly, entertaining, and effective technique. The aesthetically inclined visitor searching for stimulating and refreshing bits of color and design in an environment not primarily consecrated to art will find in the Exposition palaces many other proofs of the service which art can render in a sphere too often detached by the public from the creative artist.

It is to be hoped that many of these decorations, several of them done under great pressure, will be salvaged either as a whole or in part, to become permanently installed in some public edifice. Several of the artists undoubtedly should appreciate an opportunity to reconsider their work for permanent use more carefully, after the Exposition has closed. It would thus serve us as a reminder of the Exposition and be also a living testimony of our appreciation of an interest in our California painters in terms of a noble art, unexcelled for decorating public and private buildings. Moreover, as time passes, these manifestations of art will serve in documenting the evolution of art on the Pacific Coast and as a gauge by which to measure the standards of taste of bygone days.

DANCE OF LIFE, DETAIL—TEMPLES OF THE EAST

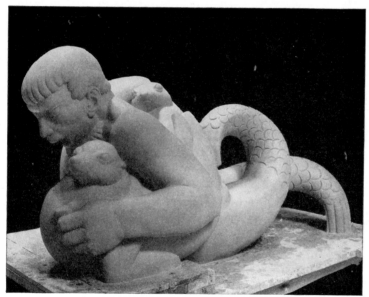

FOUNTAIN FIGURE—RAINBOW FOUNTAIN

121

Chapter VII

NIGHT EFFECTS AT THE FAIR

IN ITS DAY the illumination of the Panama-Pacific International Exposition of 1915 set a new high mark in artistic effectiveness, and it is still regarded in some respects as a criterion for exposition lighting. However, the Golden Gate International Exposition presents an entirely new technical perfection in illumination replete with beauty, which will pass into exposition history as a distinguished achievement.

In discussing this notable contribution to the enjoyment of the Exposition one must again make grateful acknowledgment of the contribution of the architect, the horticulturist, the plastic worker, and the director of color, who provided the background for the work of the illuminating expert (Dickinson). Their work appears to have been considered in advance for its adaptability to the new technical processes of lighting and the artistic effects so successfully created. In 1915, white floodlights, concealed on the tops of buildings, created an enchanting picture of a bright moonlight night. The Palace of Fine Arts (Maybeck) in particular, at night created an impression romantic and fascinating, still remembered by many after nearly twenty-five years.

The occasional use of colored gelatin did not change the fact that the illumination in 1915 was just what the work implies: bringing objects at night into light. Illumination was as yet incapable of creating color harmonies resulting from a definite palette of several different colors.

A multitude of new technical devices, such as fluorescent light—an intimate discussion of which belongs in a technical work and is outside the scope of this book—has caused a purely monochromatic lighting to be abandoned for a wide range of color harmonies and contrasts.

It is, however, apparent that from a purely artistic point of view the new technique sometimes does seem occasionally to run away with itself—simply does things because they are technically possible and not because they are essentially beautiful. There is something to be said for light at night without the addition of color other than that contributed by the surfaces on which the light is thrown; but the Exposition visitor will have to settle that personal problem according to his own aesthetic responses. However, variety of color, even though lacking in harmony, makes for gaiety; and since an exposition is to create pleasurable excitement rather than promote an introspective mood, some discordant and excessive color notes must be accepted. For an appreciation of the present Exposition at night a single comprehensive statement is not adequate, and again the Fair must be considered in terms of the several contiguous courts and open areas in which it was conceived.

On the west front of the Exposition, white light has been employed to create an effect of a moonlit city. Since it seemed desirable to make Treasure Island at night clearly visible from the San Francisco shore, white light with its greater effectiveness was indicated for the illumination of the outside walls. The effect from San Francisco under these conditions is indeed that of a magical city floating on the waters of the Bay. This alluring picture has been achieved by suppression of all glaring and distracting lights on the causeway and on the approaches on Yerba Buena Island, allowing the main buildings at night to appear as a detached, separate light unit.

At night the main tower rises above this white city in a glow of warm light that becomes whiter as it ascends in a rising crescendo, quickening its formal rhythms, culminating in great brilliance of light on the spire crowned by the golden Phoenix.

The lighting effect on the west side has been accomplished by projectors regularly spaced and concealed in troughs or trenches that run close to the base of the buildings. These are ingeniously screened by planting and in the daytime are not visible. Here we may revel in two of the most fascinating of the Exposition's light pictures, the illumi-

INDIA—COURT OF PACIFICA

nation of the major and minor elephant gates. Through the use of light thrown at opposing angles from below, the cubistic architecture here assumes at night new meaning and reveals surprising and fascinating geometrical designs. These synthetic patterns are not a part of what has been built, but a result of cross currents of light projected upward upon the flat architectural surfaces—shadow patterns which at intersections are resolved into striking optical triangular forms bold in outline and revealing unexpected gradations in intensity.

The ambitious architectural units convincingly justify themselves at night: their spatial rhythms, which seem in daylight somewhat indissoluble, then become articulated and clarified by the use of light beams. The conscious avoidance of curvilinear forms even on the elephants gives to the light here a precise quality which functions without relying upon those accidental effects which often are caused by nebulous and undefined forms.

Within the courts, the picture changes to a series of more suggestive and varied color spectacles, artistically most effective, conjuring up a variety of moods. Each court is, so to speak, a separate stage upon which color performs its magic. Each court, as in the daytime, is dominated by a definite harmony which gives to it an individual mood, and which intensifies its daytime color and architectural forms by the use of controlled colored light. A picture thus created is different from a sunlit one because of the framing by a night sky and the obscuration of all those diverting natural surroundings, such as a blue sky or a cloud pattern, which by day add an artistic element to man's own creations.

The central Court of Honor, largely devoid of color in the daytime except for the warm quality of the stucco and the color supplied by planting, at night is dominated by a feeling of warmth created by amber light from a row of lighting standards. Warmer amber light of greater chromatic intensity emanates from the belvederes and the lower part of the tower. The four fountains at the corners are accentuated by concealed sharper light beams. The general effect of this court at night maintains its sense of spaciousness and grandeur, impressive and dignified at the same time.

The Court of the Moon and Stars becomes at night a dreamy moon-lit garden, a veritable chapter from the *Arabian Nights*. The lighting here is soft and caressing, the shadows deep and mysterious. The total effect is somewhat sentimental, in keeping with the generally romantic character of this enchanting garden. The many decorative urns standing on the coping of the pool add a sharper, clearer accent, intensified by the numerous somber yews which rise solemnly at regular intervals along the edge of the basin, which at night is spanned by the arched forms created by fountains. Blue-greens and purples predominate at night as they do in the daytime.

The colors applied to the architecture are helpful in carrying the illumination into a harmony of infinite and subtle gradations of color, mostly chosen from the cooler side of the spectrum. The towers which flank the southern end seem particularly enchanting as they recede toward the top in a curious translucent glow produced by pale blue and pale green light accentuated by strong color spots in niches and wall basins. This court no doubt exerts an attraction which most visitors, particularly at the end of a strenuous day, find hard to resist: a combination of mystery, enchantment, and romance.

The open sunken garden south of the Court of the Moon and Stars inherits at night something of the romantic qualities of its neighbor. Here, the central pool with its numerous fountains is a luminous accent articulated by green lighting. The masses of oaks and shrubs at the four corners are lighted from within and hung with lanterns of the sort popularly known as "happy lanterns." Because this area is an open one, and so that it will not detract from the main group of buildings, the garden is not permitted to be spectacular at night. As the one area in the Exposition given over to outdoor recreation and to rest, and rather remote from buildings, the Enchanted Garden at night, even more than in the daytime, attracts those visitors who seek quiet.

We now retrace our steps to the central court and from there to the Court of Reflections. This latter court takes its cue from the coral walls of its daytime coloring, which in a general way is warm in contradiction to the cool tints prevailing in the Court of the Moon and Stars.

SOUTH AMERICAN FISHERMAN—COURT OF PACIFICA

SOUTH SEA ISLANDER—COURT OF PACIFICA

The walls are bathed in a warm, placid light, which is at its greatest intensity at the base and gradually fades into a lower intensity at the top of the walls.

The great triumphal arch between this court and the Court of Flowers is brought out quite boldly by lights concealed on the roofs of adjacent buildings, and the result is an architectural picture of great dignity. The large, tubular, suspended lighting standards radiating a warm glow are a very effective decorative feature in this court, as in many other places.

In the Court of Flowers the striking accents at night are the illuminated fountains against the depth of the rear walls within the arcade, with silhouettes of the arches making a dignified repeated pattern all around. Water here is never still and adds its stimulating sounds to the atmosphere of exuberance and joyousness. Memories of Granada with its overflowing basins, its gentle plashes of water ever seeking lower levels, come back to the mind of the traveler.

Conforming to the procedure followed in the discussion of other features of the Exposition, we now return to the central court and thence into the Court of the Seven Seas. This court in general has an apricot color combined with a harmonious analogous light yellow on the set-back sections of the walls. The niches decorated with sculptural sailing vessels are impregnated with fluorescent paint, so that under an invisible ultraviolet light produced by concealed projectors these decorative designs become luminous, creating against the walls behind them shadows of great depth and striking design. The commanding sculptural features of this court, the sixteen prows on the pylons, are accentuated by what is technically termed spot lighting, resulting in a pleasant reiteration of a very decorative feature. The lighting standards rising from architectural forms suggestive of maritime motives provide the accents necessary to relieve the court's extraordinary length.

The Court of Pacifica, probably the most spectacular in the daytime, is probably also the most impressive and dramatic in effect at night. Sixteen tremendous cylindrical lanterns provide the general illumination of this great court, giving it warmth and bringing together into a great harmony all the other separate lighting elements. The statue of Pacifica against its metallic curtain and a background of changing colors gains enormously under a concentrated spotlight, which creates on it new abstract patterns of light and dark not present in the daytime. The fountain in the center reveals changing colors which here create an endless succession of fascinating variations. The colossal mural on the west side also benefits from the artificial illumination; the plastic values seem more significant at night, and its color achieves a new harmony that is plainly the result of the illumination.

The entire area comprising the east walls and the adjacent territory is treated at night as a unit with a lighting scheme of a pink and golden hue. The general effect is one of mystery relieved by occasional accents to relieve monotony. Here, the two east towers contribute an emotionally effective single unit. Their color reflects something of the richness of the Orient, and this at night becomes more mysterious and suggestive through the agency of artificial light. Seen from across the waters of the lagoon, the effect is most impressive.

One cannot help but feel that night at Treasure Island is a heightened expression of all the romantic formal and color qualities that are so charming and stimulating in the daytime. At night, moreover, a more intimate feeling prevails, since natural illumination normally is absent and nature is excluded from its share in the spectacle. The blue of a California sky, the purplish hazes of the distant shore, are merely recalled at night in the twinkling of stars overhead and myriads of lights around the Bay. The illumination expert here assumes the dignity of a new creative profession; his art is no longer a mere accidental flourish upon the other arts. Fortunately, the temptation to indulge in lighting stunts for their own sake has been avoided, and lighting has been used in aiding the interpretation of the architecture and its associated arts.

Of course, searchlights and fireworks have a place in the night picture of the Exposition, and new and unusual ideas are carried out, particularly in taking advantage of the great lagoon and its large mir-

NORTH AMERICAN WOMAN—COURT OF PACIFICA

roring surfaces. Besides, innumerable pictures are created that are not always the result of deliberate planning—so much that is aesthetically pleasing results from the inadvertence of happy accident.

Light, which since the Impressionist painters has played such an important part in pictorial art, has exerted itself in innumerable ways, perhaps not always pleasing, but at any rate gay and refreshing. A leisurely stroll in the vicinity of the great lagoon and its extensions is quite sufficient to vindicate this contention. The trees and buildings silhouetted against a night sky summon up suggestive forms of exotic origin, doubly so as they are reflected in the placid waters. Here, perhaps, one receives some compensation for the neglect of drawing the waters of the Bay into closer harmony with this walled city. It is at night that one particularly feels the charm and mystery of the water with its illusive distances and depths.

The annoying blatancy of "Neon" light, undoubtedly effective in advertising, has been relegated to the Gayway area, which thrives on the exploiting of the lower aspects of human requirements.

CONCLUSION

WHEN the lights are finally extinguished at Treasure Island, the Exposition will take its place with other memories of the past without leaving in its wake a sense of fatigue or mental confusion, as some recent expositions have done. As a thing of beauty, it will be a joy forever, to be reëxperienced in retrospect. It will serve as a lasting reminder that this enchanting spectacle represents a special world made accessible to us by the artist, a world which, though evanescent and temporary, reveals glimpses of beauty that must carry us through the long moments of tedium of everyday existence.

We should always remember also that the love of form and color which is so prodigally displayed at the Exposition suggests something of the general character of California. Color proves one of the dominant contributions of this undertaking, and this is quite natural, because color is the keynote of the Pacific Slope, and no less so of the Orient, which also is an integral part of the picture.

The ultimate significance of this Exposition, apart from its emphasis upon artistic values, is that it will also contribute socially to the West. People who can surrender themselves so freely and wholeheartedly to celebrations possess a special capacity for richer living—a capacity that is to be admired and kept alive. To translate this capacity into outwardly visible and aesthetically enjoyable forms is equally important, and from that task San Francisco and the West should never shrink. It is life translated into its noblest equivalents.

VASE AND PANEL, HALL OF WESTERN STATES

Appendix I

BIOGRAPHICAL NOTES

NOTES on the architects, sculptors, painters, and others who have contributed to the art of Treasure Island, together with their contributions

BALLIN, HUGO. Painter, Pacific Palisades, San Monica Bay, Calif. Born, New York City, 1879. Studied at Art Students League, New York; three years in Italy, Florence, Rome. Two murals, "The Winds," in the Arch of the Winds, between the Court of Reflections and the Court of Flowers.

BERGMANN, FRANZ W. Painter, San Francisco. Born, Vienna, 1898. Studied at the Kunstakademie, Vienna. Two murals, "Gold" and "Fortuna," in the western south tower of the Court of the Moon and Stars; four murals, "Vanity," "The Bible," "The Coming of Peace," and "Religion on the Pacific Coast," in the Temple of Religion.

BERLANDINA, JANE. Born, Nice, 1898. Training: Ecole Nationale des Arts Décoratifs, Paris. Mural, "The Spiritual and Material Joys of San Francisco: Ballet, Food, Opera, Symphony," in the San Francisco Building. Murals, "Agriculture and Natural Resources of Brazil," in the Pavilion of Brazil.

BESSE, GEORGES. Architecte du Gouvernement, Paris. Born, Paris, 1900. Training: Ecole Nationale des Beaux-Arts. Grand Prix de Rome. (With Claude Meyer-Lévy) Pavilions of France and French Indo-China, Palace of Elegance.

BOLLES, EDWARD G. Architect, San Francisco. Born, Berkeley, 1905. Training: University of Oklahoma, B.S.; Harvard University, M.A.; archaeological work in Anatolia, Egypt, Persia, Yucatan. Temple of Religion. Christian Science Activities Building.

BORN, ERNEST ALEXANDER. Architect, painter, San Francisco. Born, San Francisco, 1898. Training: University of California, A.B., and study abroad. San Joaquin and Alta California Building. Design of directional mural maps at the entrances to the Exposition. Mural, "The Industries of the San Francisco Area," in the San Francisco Building.

BRAGHETTA, LULU HAWKINS. Sculptor, San Francisco. Born, Santa Ana, Calif. Training: University of Nevada, B.A.; University of California, M.A.; Art Students League, Metropolitan School of Art, Grand Central Art School of New York. Relief, "Darkness," on wall of southern Temple of the East.

BROWN, JR., ARTHUR. Architect, San Francisco. Born, Oakland, Calif., 1874. Training: University of California, B.S., LL.D.; Ecole Nationale des Beaux-Arts, Paris. Chairman, Architectural Commission of the Exposition (succeeding George W. Kelham, December, 1936). Court of Honor. Tower of the Sun.

BRUTON, ESTHER. Painter. Born, Alameda, Calif. Studied at Art Students League, New York, under Bridgeman. (With Helen and Margaret Bruton) Mural, "Pacific Relations," on the west wall of the Court of Pacifica.

BRUTON, HELEN. Painter. Born, Alameda, Calif. (With Esther and Margaret Bruton) Mural in the Court of Pacifica.

139

BRUTON, MARGARET. Painter. Born, Brooklyn, N.Y. Studied at Art Students League, New York, under Robert Henri. (With Helen and Esther Bruton) Mural in the Court of Pacifica.

CADORIN, ETTORE. Sculptor, San Francisco. Born, Venice, 1876. Studied in his father's studio and at the Royal Academy of Fine Arts, Venice. Statues: "Earth," in the Court of Honor; "The Evening Star," in the Court of the Moon and Stars; "Moon and the Dawn," in the Enchanted Garden.

CANALI, PIETRO. Architect. Consultant, Pavilion of Italy.

CARLTON, BRENTS. Sculptor, San Francisco. Born, Roswell, N.M., 1903. Training: California School of Fine Arts. Two statues, "Polynesians," in the Court of Pacifica. Two figures in bas-relief on the California Building.

CARTER, DUDLEY. Sculptor, Carmel, Calif. Born, New Westminster, B.C., 1892. Studied for a short period at the Seattle Art Institute and at the Cornish School of Art; largely self-taught. Wood carvings on the doors of the Shasta-Cascade Building.

CHAMBERS, HAROLD C. Architect, Los Angeles. Born, Hampton, Neb., 1885. Studied at the Armour Institute of Technology, Chicago. Southern Counties Building.

COVARRUBIAS, MIGUEL. Painter, illustrator, caricaturist. Born, Mexico City, 1904. Self-taught. Six illustrated maps, "Peoples," "Flora and Fauna," "Economy," "Art and Culture," "Housing," and "Transportation" of the people of the Pacific Area, in Pacific House.

CRAVATH, RUTH. Sculptor, San Francisco. Born, Chicago, 1902. Studied at the California School of Fine Arts under Ralph Stackpole and Beniamino Bufano. Fountain group, "North America," in the Court of Pacifica.

DAILEY, GARDNER A. Architect, San Francisco. Born, St. Paul, Minn., 1895. Pavilion of Brazil.

DANIELS, MARK. Architect, landscape designer, San Francisco. Born, Jackson, Mich., 1881. Training: University of California, B.S.; postgraduate work at Harvard University. Landscape architect for the California Commission and the Federal Building, Southern Counties Building, Chinese Village, and the Hall of Flowers.

D'ANS, ARMANDO. Architect, Buenos Aires. Born, Buenos Aires, 1912. Training: School of Architecture, Buenos Aires. Pavilion of Argentina.

DEICHMAN, O. A. Architect, San Francisco. Born, Germany, 1890. Training: San Francisco Architectural Club, and offices. The Shasta-Cascade Building and Court.

DELA CRUZ, PABLO. Architect. (With Rafael Ruiz) Pavilion of Colombia.

DEL PINO, JOSÉ MOYA. Painter, San Francisco. Born, Cordoba, Spain, 1891. Training: Academy of Fine Arts, Madrid; Academie Colarossi, Paris. Mural, "Spanish Fiesta," in the California Building. Mural, "Man in Relation to God," in the Hall of Religion.

DEPPE, ROBERT. Architect, Batavia, Java. Born, Amsterdam, 1902. Training: School for Decorative Arts, Trade School for Building Arts, School for Industrial Arts, School of Architecture, Amsterdam. Pavilion of the Netherland East Indies.

DICKERSON, A. F. Manager, illuminating laboratory, General Electric Company, Schenectady, N. Y. Born, Cuero, Texas, 1888. Training: Texas Agricultural and Mechanical College, B.S., E.E. Illumination engineer.

PAVILION OF BRAZIL

141

DIXON, MAYNARD. Painter, San Francisco. Born, Fresno, 1875. Self-educated in art. Two murals, "Plowed Land" and "Grass Land," in the Court of Pacifica.

EDMONDSON, HAROLD ALFRED. Architect. Born, Lovelock, Nev., 1899. Training: University of California, B.S.; under George Washington Smith, Santa Barbara, and Robert D. Farquhar, Los Angeles. (With Robert Stanton) Mission Trails Building.

FORBES, HELEN KATHERINE. Painter, San Francisco. Born, San Francisco, 1891. Studied at San Francisco School of Art under Frank Van Sloan, at Monterey under Armin Hansen, at Munich under Groeber, and at Paris under L'Hôte. Two murals, "The First Garden," in the eastern south tower of the Court of the Moon and Stars.

FRICK, EDWARD LOUIS. Architect, San Francisco. Born, San Francisco, 1891. Training: Ecole Nationale des Beaux-Arts, Paris. Assistant to Arthur Brown, Jr., in the Court of Honor and the Tower of the Sun. Chief of the Division of Architecture in the Exposition's Department of Works. Designer, Hall of Western States, Latin American group, exterior façades of the additions to the Fine Arts Building, Aviation Building, bridges, kiosks, and other similar embellishments throughout the grounds.

GEORGE, CARL. Sculptor, San Francisco. Born, Des Moines, Iowa, 1908. Studied at the California School of Fine Arts under Ralph Stackpole, Maurice Sterne, and others. Two statues representing "North America," in the Court of Pacifica.

GERRITY, JOHN EMMETT. Painter, Berkeley. Born, Mountain View, Calif., 1895. Studied by himself. Decorations in the Temple of Religion (Constance Woolsey, assistant).

GIROD, JULIUS LÉON. Horticulturist, landscape engineer, Senior Assistant Superintendent of Parks, City and County of San Francisco. Born, San Francisco, 1900. Studied under John McLaren. Chief of the Exposition's Bureau of Horticulture.

GOULD, ELMER G. Landscape architect. Born, Soledad, Calif., 1910. Deputy Chief, Bureau of Horticulture.

GRAHAM, CECILIA BANCROFT. Sculptor, San Francisco. Born, San Francisco, 1905. Graduate, Mills College. Studied sculpture in Vienna under Oscar Thiede; also at Rome and Paris, and under Carl Milles at Granbrook Academy, Michigan. Three statues, "South America" group, in the Court of Pacifica. Two fountain figures in the oval court of the San Francisco Building.

GUTIERREZ, GREGORIO P. Architect, Manila, P. I. Born, Manila, 1908. Training: Massachusetts Institute of Technology, Cambridge; Ecole Nationale des Beaux-Arts, Paris; Fontainebleau School of Art. Pavilion of the Philippines.

HANSEN, ARMIN CARL. Painter, etcher, Monterey, Calif. Born, San Francisco, 1886. Training: Mark Hopkins Institute of Art, San Francisco; Royal Academy, Stuttgart, Germany; and in Belgium. Six panels over doors in the Court of the Seven Seas.

HILER, HILAIRE. Painter. Born, St. Paul, Minn., 1898. Self-taught abroad, Paris. Two illustrated maps, "Exploration," "Countries of the Pacific," in Pacific House.

HOBART, LEWIS PARSONS. Architect, San Francisco. Born, St. Louis, Mo., 1873. Studied: University of California, American Academy at Rome, Beaux-Arts Institute of Design, Paris. Member, Architectural Commission of the Exposition. Court of Reflections, Arch of the Winds, Court of Flowers, Rainbow Fountain. Consulting architect, Pavilion of Hawaii.

HOWARD, HENRY T. Architect, San Francisco. Born, New York, 1894. Training: University of California, A.B., M.A.; Ecole Nationale des Beaux-Arts, Paris. Sacramento Valley-Tahoe Region Building, in the California group.

HOWARD, ROBERT BOARDMAN. Painter, sculptor, San Francisco. Born, New York, 1896. Pupil of Perham Nahl, Xavier Martínez, Kenneth Hayes Miller. Vases and relief in Hall of Western States. Fountain group in the San Francisco Building. Murals on the Pavilion of Brazil. Decorative parrot on the Ghirardelli Building. Three reliefs on the California Auditorium. Decorative maps in the grand hall of the California Building.

HUFF, WILLIAM GORDON. Sculptor, Berkeley. Born, Fresno, Calif., 1903. Studied at the California School of Arts and Crafts (College of Arts and Crafts), Oakland; California School of Fine Arts, San Francisco; Art Students League, New York; Ecole Grande Chaumière, Paris. Figure on the Arch of the Winds (repeated); figure in the Court of Flowers (repeated). Four large standing figures, "Science," "Agriculture," "Industry," "Art," in the Court of Honor.

HUNTINGTON, ANNA HYATT. Sculptor, New York. Born, Cambridge, Mass., 1876. Training: Art Students League, New York; pupil of H. A. McNeil and Gutzon Borglum. Statue, "St. Francis," on the south lawn of the Court of Honor.

JOHNSON, SARGENT CLAUDE. Sculptor, Berkeley. Born, Boston, 1898. Studied at Worcester Art School, Worcester, Mass.; California School of Fine Arts, San Francisco; also with Beniamino Bufano. Two statues, "Inca Indian and Llama," in the Court of Pacifica. Three statues, symbolizing "Industry," "Home Life," and "Agriculture," in the Alameda-Contra Costa Building.

KELHAM, GEORGE WILLIAM. Architect, San Francisco. Born, Manchester, Mass., 1871; died, San Francisco, 1936. Studied architecture at Harvard, and at Paris and Rome. Chairman of the Exposition's Architectural Commission, June, 1935 to December, 1936. Court of the Moon and Stars. Court of the Seven Seas. (With W. P. Day) Administration Building, Aviation Hangars.

KENT, ADELINE. Sculptor, San Francisco. Born, Kentfield, Calif., 1900. Studied at the California School of Fine Arts. Two relief figures, in the Court of Honor. Group of three figures, "Islands of the Pacific," on the central fountain in the Court of Pacifica.

KNOWLES, SQUIRE. Painter. Born, Hanford, Calif., 1901. Training: University of California, A.B.; California School of Fine Arts. Mural decoration for the California Packing Corporation exhibit, in the Food Palace.

LABAUDT, LUCIEN. Painter, San Francisco. Born, Paris, 1880. Self-taught. Mural, "Art and Industries of California," on the façade of the California Building. Mural, "Agriculture," on the façade of the California Auditorium.

MACKY, DONALD. Sculptor, San Francisco. Born, San Francisco, 1913. Training: California School of Fine Arts; offices, Bakewell and Weihe. Elephant groups on the Portals of the Pacific.

MALMQUIST, OLOF C. Sculptor, San Francisco. Born, Wallingford, Conn., 1894. Training: Under Lee Lawrie, sculptor, Yale; American Academy at Rome. Two bears for the California Building. Models for "Phoenix," "The Winds," "Signs of the Zodiac," symbolic heads "Water," "Earth," on the Tower of the Sun. Model for statue, "Fauna," in the Court of Honor. Models for fountain figures, "The Rainbow" and aquatic groups, in the Court of Flowers.

Grau photo

ENTRANCE, SHASTA-CASCADE BUILDING

MAYBECK, BERNARD RALPH. Architect, San Francisco. Born, New York, 1862. Student: Ecole Nationale et Spéciale des Beaux-Arts, Ecole des Beaux-Arts, Arts et Métiers, Paris. (With William G. Merchant) Redwood Empire Building, Temples of the East.

MAYHEW, CLARENCE W. Architect, San Francisco. Born, Denver, Colo., 1907. Training: University of Illinois, University of California. Dairy Council Building.

MERCHANT, WILLIAM GLADSTONE. Architect, San Francisco. Born in Sonoma County, Calif., 1893. Training: offices of John Galen Howard and of Maybeck and White. Pacific House. (With Bernard R. Maybeck) Temples of the East, Redwood Empire Building.

MEYER-LÉVY, CLAUDE. Architect, Paris (P. and G. Meyer-Lévy). Born, Paris, 1908. Training: Ecole Nationale des Beaux-Arts, Paris. (In collaboration with Georges Besse) Pavilion of France.

MORROW, IRVING F. Architect, San Francisco. Born, Oakland, Calif., 1884. Training: University of California; Ecole Nationale des Beaux-Arts, Paris; offices of John Galen Howard, William G. Hays, John T. Donovan, Louis Christian Mullgardt. Alameda-Contra Costa Building, in the California group.

OLMSTED, FREDERICK. Sculptor, San Francisco. Born, San Francisco, 1911. Training: California School of Fine Arts, and abroad. Five figures on the California Building.

PATIGIAN, HAIG. Sculptor, San Francisco. Born, Van, Armenia, 1876. Almost entirely self-taught. Four single figures, "Earth Dormant," "Sunshine," "Rain," and "Harvest," in the Enchanted Garden. Group, "Creation," in the Court of Seven Seas.

PFLUEGER, TIMOTHY L. Architect, San Francisco. Born, San Francisco, 1892. Training: in architects' offices and at the Beaux-Arts Institute of Design, Paris. Member of the Architectural Commission of the Exposition, and supervising architect, California Commission. Federal Building. Court of Pacifica. California Building. California Auditorium. Supervising architect, Netherland East Indies Pavilion.

PHILLIPS, HELEN ELIZABETH. Sculptor, San Francisco. Born, Fresno, Calif., 1913. Studied at the California School of Fine Arts. Group of three fountain figures in the Court of Pacifica.

POOLE, HORATIO NELSON. Painter, San Francisco. Born, Haddenfield, N.J., 1885. Studied at the Pennsylvania Academy of Fine Arts. Two murals, "California at Play" and "California at Work," in the western south tower of the Court of the Moon and Stars.

POULSON, MAGNUS. Architect, Oslo, Norway. Born, Oslo, 1885. Norway Building.

PUCCINELLI, DOROTHY WAGNER. Painter, San Francisco. Born, San Antonio, Tex., 1901. Studied under Rudolph Schaeffer at the California School of Fine Arts, and at the School of Design, San Francisco. Two panels in oil on canvas, "The First Garden," in the eastern south tower of the Court of the Moon and Stars.

PUCCINELLI, RAYMOND. Sculptor, San Francisco. Born, San Francisco, 1904. Studied under Rudolph Schaeffer at the California School of Fine Arts, and in Europe. Five standing figures for the San Francisco Building. Statue, "Flora," in the Court of Honor.

RUIZ, ANTONIO. Born, Mexico City, 1897. Training: School of Fine Arts, Mexico City; assistant to Miguel Covarrubias.

RUIZ, RAFAEL. Architect. (With Pablo Dela Cruz) Pavilion of Colombia.

SAKURAI, NAGAO. Landscape architect, Tokyo. Japanese Garden.

SCHNIER, JACQUES. Sculptor, San Francisco. Born, Constanza, Roumania, 1898. Training: Stanford University, engineering; University of California, architecture; afterwards studied sculpture. Two statues, "Ocean Breeze" and "High Sierra," on the balcony of the Towers of the East. Bas-relief, "Dance of Life," on the northern Tower of the East. Two statues, representing "The Spirit of India," on the central fountain in the Court of Pacifica. Eagles on the Arch of the Winds. Reliefs, "East" and "West," over the entrance near the Administration Building.

SHEETS, MILLARD. Painter, Claremont, Calif. Born, Pomona, Calif., 1907. Pupil of Chovinard School of Art, Los Angeles. Six murals, "Spanish Era," "Gold Era," "Modern Era," "Daytime in Agriculture," "Clock Time in Industry," and "Infinite Time," in the Court of Flowers. Panel, "Horn of Plenty," on the Southern Counties Building. Four panels, "The Importance of Recreation in Society," on the California Building.

SHEPHERD, HARRY WHITCOMB. Landscape architect, Berkeley. Born, Attleboro, Mass., 1890. Training: University of California, B.S.; study abroad. Garden court of the Alameda-Contra Costa Building.

SIMPSON, MARIAN. Painter, Berkeley. Born, Kansas City, Mo., 1899. Training: Cleveland School of Art, Paris, Spain. Two panels, "Rural Life," "Urban Life," in the Alameda-Contra Costa Building.

SLIVKA, DAVID. Sculptor, San Francisco. Born, Chicago, 1913. Studied at the California School of Fine Arts. Panels, "Abundance" and "Fertility," on the east walls of the Court of Honor. Decorative figure in relief on urn in the Court of Reflection.

SOTOMAYOR, ANTONIO. Sculptor, painter. Born, Bolivia, 1904. Training: Art School, La Paz; San Francisco School of Art. Terra-cotta relief map in Pacific House. Murals, "Life in Pre-Columbian Peru," in the Pavilion of Peru.

SPENCER, ELDRIDGE T. Architect (Spencer, Blanchard and Maher), San Francisco. Born, 1893, Woodland, Calif. Training: University of California, Ecole Nationale des Beaux-Arts. Associate architect, French Building, French Indo-China Building, Palace of Elegance.

STACKPOLE, RALPH. Sculptor, San Francisco. Born, Williams, Ore., 1885. Studied under Arthur Putnam and Gottardo Piazzoni, San Francisco, and at the Ecole Nationale des Beaux-Arts, Paris. Statue, "Pacifica," in the Court of Pacifica.

STANTON, JESS. Architect, color consultant, San Francisco. Born, San Francisco, 1887. Training: in art schools and architects' offices in San Francisco, Chicago, and New York, under Maybeck, Pissis, Burnham, Hobart, and others. The Exposition's Director of Color, in charge of color, decoration, and night lighting.

STANTON, ROBERT. Architect, Del Monte, Calif. Born, Detroit, Mich., 1901. Training: University of California, and in offices, Los Angeles. Associate architect, Mission Trails Building.

STIEHL, CLAUDE ALBON. Architect, Honolulu, T. H. Born, San Francisco, 1902. Training: Armour Institute of Technology, Chicago, B.S. Pavilion of Hawaii.

STOLL, JOHN (THEODOR EDWARD). Painter, etcher, San Francisco. Born, Göttingen, Germany, 1898. Studied at Dresden, Germany; largely self-taught. Six murals, "Horizons," "4 P.M.: Southwest Wind Increasing to a Gale," "Hold Her," "Took in All Head Sails," "Blew out Lower Topsail," "8 A.M.: Took in Foresail," in the Court of the Seven Seas.

THE PEACEMAKERS—COURT OF PACIFICA

SUSINI, ALFIO. Architect, Rome. Born, Cairo, Egypt, 1900. Training: School of Architecture, Rome. Pavilion of Italy.

TALIABUE, CARLO. Sculptor, San Francisco. Born, Cremona, Italy, 1894. Training, Royal Academy of Art, Milan. Figures representing "The Spirit of Travel" and "Transportation," on the south façade of the Aviation Building. Statue, "Sea," in the Court of Honor.

TAMURA, TAKESHI. Landscape architect, Tokyo. Gardens of the Japanese area.

TANTAU, CLARENCE A. Architect, San Francisco. Born, San Francisco, 1884. Studied in architects' offices in San Francisco and abroad. Associate Architect of the California Commission. Interior of the San Francisco Building.

TAYLOR, EDGAR DORSEY. Artist in glass, Berkeley. Born, Grass Valley, Calif., 1904. Training: University of California, M.A.; and abroad. Leaded glass map, "Modern Trade Routes of the Pacific Area," in Pacific House.

TOGNELLI, P. O. Sculptor, San Francisco. Born in Pietra Santa, Italy, 1880. Studied at the Accademia delle Bellearti, Florence. All modeling and sculpture in the Court of the Seven Seas and the Court of the Moon and Stars.

TOGNELLI, WILLIAM. Sculptor, son of P. O. Tognelli. Born, San Francisco, 1905. Studied at the San Francisco School of Fine Arts. Assistant to his father in Exposition work.

TOKI, TATUNAO. Architect, Tokyo. Associate architect, Pavilion of Japan.

UTIDA, YOSHIZO. Architect, Tokyo. Pavilion of Japan.

VOLTZ, HERMAN. Painter. Born, Zurich, Switzerland, 1904. Studied in Vienna, Austria; largely self-taught. Mural, "Conquest of the West by Land and by Water," on the Federal Building (carried out as a Federal Art Project exhibit).

VON MEYER, MICHAEL. Sculptor, San Francisco. Born, Odessa, Russia, 1894. Studied at the Academy of Art, Odessa, and at the California School of Fine Arts. Bas-reliefs, "Beauty," "Knowledge," "Music," and "Labor," in the Court of Reflections.

WALTER, EDGAR. Sculptor, San Francisco. Born, San Francisco, 1877; died, 1938. Studied in Paris. Statue, "Penguin Girl," in the west basin of the Court of Reflections.

WEIHE, ERNEST E. Architect (Bakewell and Weihe), San Francisco. Born, California, 1893. Studied at the Beaux-Arts Institute of Design of America and at the Ecole Nationale des Beaux-Arts, Paris. Member, Architectural Commission of the Exposition. West façades, including the Portals of the Pacific.

WURSTER, WILLIAM WILSON. Architect, San Francisco. Born, Stockton, Calif., 1895. Training: University of California (architecture), and in architectural offices, New York. Yerba Buena Clubhouse. Associate architect (with Armando D'Ans), Pavilion of the Argentine.

YOUTZ, PHILIP NEWELL. Architect, museum director. Born, Quincy, Mass., 1895. Training: Amherst College, B.A.; Oberlin College, M.A. Consultant and Architectural Director, the Pacific Area.

THE FIRST GARDEN—SOUTH TOWERS

APPENDIX II

IMPORTANT EXPOSITIONS

A CHRONOLOGICAL LIST of the more important world's fairs and international and commemorative expositions held since 1851

Exposition of the Industry of All Nations	London	1851
World's Fair	New York	1853
International Exposition	Munich	1854
International Exposition	Paris	1855
World's Fair	London	1862
International Exposition	Paris	1867
International Universal Exposition	Vienna	1873
The Centennial Exposition	Philadelphia	1876
International Exposition of Art and Industry	Paris	1878
International Exposition	Sidney	1879
World's Fair	Melbourne	1880
Invention Exposition	London	1885
Paris Universal Exposition	Paris	1889
World's Columbian Exposition	Chicago	1893
California Midwinter Exposition*	San Francisco	1894
International Exposition	Paris	1900
Pan-American Exposition	Buffalo	1901
Louisiana Purchase Exposition	St. Louis	1904
Lewis and Clark Centennial Exposition	Portland, Ore.	1905
National Exposition Commemorating the First Century of [Brazilian] Independence	Rio de Janeiro	1908
Alaska-Yukon Exposition	Seattle	1909
National Exposition	Quito	1909
Panama-Pacific International Exposition	San Francisco	1915
National Exposition of Panama	Panama	1916
Panama-California International Exposition	San Diego	1916
British Empire Exposition	Wembly	1924
International Centennial Exposition	La Paz	1925
A Century of Progress Exposition	Chicago	1933
Texas Centennial Exposition	Dallas	1936

* Noted here because it was the first international exposition held west of the Rocky Mountains.

THE FIRST GARDEN—SOUTH TOWERS

157

PLANTING LISTS

THESE LISTS of the horticultural material used at Treasure Island, giving botanical and popular names, were put at my disposal by Mr. J. L. Girod, and by Mr. Mark Daniels. Willis L. Jepson, Professor of Botany, Emeritus, in the University of California, has supplied the names of the countries of origin of the different plants, and has added other authoritative botanical information.

GOLD—SOUTH TOWERS

161

NORTH SQUARE COURT
(Court of Pacifica)

HORTICULTURAL COLOR SCHEME: BLUE AND GOLD

TREES AND SHRUBS

Eucalyptus globulus. A native of Australia. Two sixty-five-foot specimen trees flanking the statue of Pacifica.

Eucalyptus globulus var. *compacta.* Australia. Two twenty-foot specimen trees flanking the statue of Pacifica.

Griselinia lucida. New Zealand. Thirty-two ten-foot specimens bordering steps leading from the statue of Pacifica to the central fountain.

Acacia melanoxylon, standards. Blackwood Acacia. Australia. Sixteen formal, clipped trees around the central fountain.

Eriobotrya japonica (or, *Photinia japonica*). Loquat. China. Twenty-two large specimens at the perimeter of the court. Many in fruit and flower. Although a native of China, it is sometimes called the "Japan Plum."

Libocedrus decurrens. Incense Cedar. California. Twenty-two columnar specimen trees placed beneath the Bruton mural and bordering and opposite the Ford Building.

Ligustrum japonicum. Japan Privet. Japan. Seven large trees in the same position as the Incense Cedars.

Pittosporum undulatum. Victorian Box. Australia. Eight-foot specimens used.

Coprosma baueri (or, *Coprosma stockii*). Mirror Plant. New Zealand. Used as background at entrances to palaces. A few large specimens also used.

Laurocerasus officinalis (or, *Prunus laurocerasus*). Cherry Laurel. Native of southeastern Europe to Persia.

Veronica andersonii (or, *Hebe andersonii*). Speedwell. A garden hybrid between *H. salicifolia* and *H. speciosa,* both of which are New Zealand species. Flowers white, tipped with violet. Used as a hedge around the central fountain.

Veronica. Autumn Glory. A horticultural variety. Original stock imported from England. This is the first showing in the United States of this dark blue variety.

Juniperus chinensis var. *pfitzeriana.* Pfitzer's Juniper. One hundred and forty-eight prostrate specimens around the central fountain. A horticultural variety. *J. chinensis* is native to the Himalayas, China, and Japan; the named varieties appear to be mainly of horticultural derivation.

INITIAL PLANTING OF ANNUALS AND BULBS

Hyacinths.

Calendula. *Calendula officinalis* is from southeast Europe.

Violas.

Wallflowers.

Pansies.

Marguerites.

Poppies.

NORTH LONG COURT

(Court of the Seven Seas)

Horticultural Color Scheme: Yellow and White

TREES AND SHRUBS

Eucalyptus globulus. Australia. Forty-six specimens, ranging in height from thirty to seventy-five feet, placed against walls and under statuary on the summits of the court.

Pittosporum tenuifolium. Tawhiwhi. *Pittosporum eugenioides.* Tarata. *Pittosporum crassifolium.* Karo. All are natives of New Zealand. Specimens used, from ten to thirty feet in height.

Poplar. Twelve specimens, ranging from thirty-five to forty-five feet in height, used at sides of doorways. If this be *Populus nigra* var. *italica* (Lombardy Poplar), it is a native of Europe and Asia.

Acacia melanoxylon (or, *A. nigricans*). Blackwood Acacia. Australia. Loose specimens forming part of the wall planting.

Acacia melanoxylon, standards. Australia. Forty large Acacia standards, running down either side of this court and presenting a very formal appearance. Procured for the most part on Dolores Street in San Francisco.

Taxus baccata var. *fastigiata* (or, *T. hibernica*). Irish Yew. Four specimens, about eighteen feet high, used to flank "Discovery" in the two central entrances to this court. Horticultural variant originating in Ireland. The species is found in Europe, North Africa, and western Asia.

Other shrubs used in this court include the following:

Double White-flowering Peach Trees.

Forsythia. A native of China.

Spiraea vanhouttei.

Genista canariensis (standard horticultural name, *Cytisus canariensis*). Canary Island Broom. A native of the Canary Islands.

English Laurels.

Myrtus communis. Classical Myrtle. A native of the Mediterranean region.

Viburnum opulus sterile. Snowball Bush. Found in Europe, North Africa, Asia.

Acacia longifolia and *Acacia floribunda.* Natives of Australia.

INITIAL PLANTING OF ANNUALS AND BULBS

Lemon-yellow Poppies, Amurense.
Apricot-colored Violas.
White Violas.
Tulip Avis Kennicott, yellow.
Tulip White King.

Tulip White Superior.
Tulip Avelon.
Tulip South Pole.
White English Daisies, *Bellis perennis.*

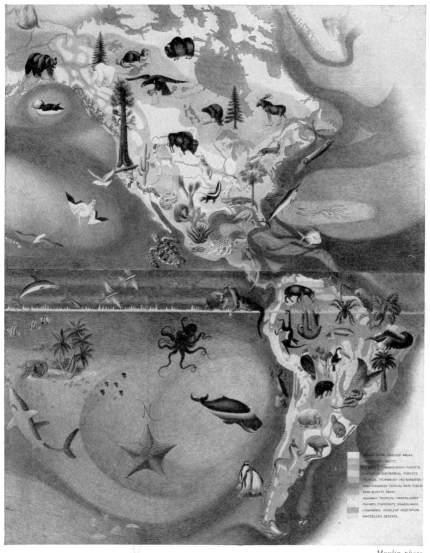

DETAIL OF MAP, THE FAUNA AND FLORA OF THE PACIFIC, PACIFIC HOUSE

CENTRAL COURT

(Court of Honor)

HORTICULTURAL COLOR SCHEME: GOLD AND BRONZE

TREES AND SHRUBS

Magnolia grandiflora (or, *M. foetida*). Bull Bay. A native of North America (North Carolina to Texas). Fifty-six large specimen trees, from twenty to forty-five feet in height, placed at the perimeter of this court.

Magnolia soulangiana. Japan. A hybrid between *M. denudata* and *M. liliflora.* One large specimen tree used in this court.

Valencia Oranges. Trees from ten to twelve feet high, and loaded with fruit, brought to the Exposition from Montebello, southern California.

Arbutus menziesii. Madroño. Pacific Coast of North America. Four large specimens from twenty to twenty-five feet in height, with a twenty-five-foot spread, used at the western base of the Tower of the Sun.

Buxus suffruticosa. Europe, North Africa, West Asia. A variety of *B. sempervirens.* More than two thousand linear feet used in this court as hedging.

Genista canariensis (or, *Cytisus canariensis*). Canary Island Broom. A native of the Canary Islands.

Azalea mollis (or, *Rhododendron molle;* or, *R. sinense*). A native of China. *Azalea altaclarensis.* A native of the Himalayas. Five hundred five-foot specimens of *Azalea mollis* are used beneath balustrades of the four loggias. Twenty-five hundred *Azalea altaclarensis* in various varieties are also used in this court.

Laurocerasus officinalis (or, *Prunus laurocerasus*). Cherry Laurel. Southeastern Europe to Persia. Used beneath balustrades of the four loggias.

Aucuba japonica var. *variegata.* Gold-dust Tree, var. *maculata.* About two hundred and fifty specimens are used under the Magnolias. A native of Asia (Himalayas to Japan); belongs to the Dogwood Family.

Otaheite Dwarf Oranges. This is *Citrus taitensis,* but not of Tahiti or Otaheite; it is a horticultural variant. The original home of ordinary Orange is China or southeastern Asia.

Piper capsicum var. *indicum.* Ornamental Pepper. Burma. Used in borders.

Lonicera nitida. Honeysuckle. Western China. Used as hedging.

INITIAL PLANTING OF FLOWERS AND BULBS

Arethusa Tulips, yellow.
Moonlight Tulips, yellow.
White Violas.
Queen of the Blues Hyacinths.

Innocence Hyacinths.
"Radio" Violas.
Lord Beaconsfield Pansies.

SOUTH COURT

(Court of the Moon and Stars)

HORTICULTURAL COLOR SCHEME: BLUE

TREES AND SHRUBS

Eucalyptus globulus. Australia. Thirty specimens, forty to seventy feet high, used against the walls.

Ceanothus thyrsiflorus. Blue Blossom, Lady Bloom. California and Oregon. Twenty ten- to twelve-foot specimens and thirty fifteen- to twenty-foot specimens used in this court.

Acacia melanoxylon (or, *A. nigricans*). Blackwood Acacia. Australia. Thirty-five tall loose specimens used as background.

Taxus baccata var. *fastigiata* (or, *T. hibernica*). Irish Yew. Europe. Fourteen twenty- to twenty-five-foot specimens used as border plants around the central pool. Also used to flank doorways.

Arbutus menziesii. Madroño. Pacific Coast of North America. Four twenty-five-foot specimens with a twenty-foot spread, planted near the Fountain of the Evening Star.

Laurocerasus officinalis (or, *Prunus laurocerasus*). Cherry Laurel. Southeastern Europe to Persia. Used behind fountain.

Ligustrum japonicum. Japan. Two fifty-foot specimens, and several smaller trees.

Umbellularia californica. California Bay. California and Oregon. A single thirty-five-foot specimen.

Cedrus atlantica. Atlas Cedar. Morocco.

Pinus radiata. Monterey Pine. California.

Pittosporum tenuifolium. New Zealand.

Cydonia candida. Flowering Quince. Japan. White form of Scarlet Japanese Flowering Quince. Used as border.

One espaliered Apple Tree.

Pleroma grandiflora (or, *Tibouchina elegans, T. semidecandra, P. macranthum, P. splendens*). Glory Bush. Brazil. Has deep purple flowers to five inches across. Used as border.

Veronica decussata (or, *Hebe elliptica;* or, *V. elliptica*). Ironweed. New Zealand. Used as a three-inch to eight-inch hedge all around lawns in this court.

Ligustrum ovalifolium (or, *L. californicum*). California Privet. Japan. In front of the *Taxus baccata* at the doorways.

Azara microphylla. A native of Chile. Twelve-foot specimens used.

Philadelphus coronarius. Mock Orange. A native of Europe and southwest Asia.

Buddleia. Summer Lilac. Most of the cultivated species are from Asia.

Hydrangea (turned to blue). The common outdoor Hydrangea is from China and Japan.

Echium bourgeanum. Viper's Bugloss. Canary Islands. Flowers rose, in dense pyramidal spikes.

Rhododendron album elegans. The botanical *R. album* is from Java.

Rhododendron album novum.

Rhododendron himalayan.

Rhododendron roseum elegans.

Rhododendron Mrs. J. Waterer.

Rhododendron blandinianum. A native of Central America.

Rhododendron Pink Pearl.

Coprosma baueri. New Zealand.

Azalea mollis. Australia.

Acacia floribunda. Australia.

Acacia longifolia. Australia.

Teucrium fruticans. Germander. Europe.

DAYTIME IN AGRICULTURE—COURT OF FLOWERS

169

SOUTH COURT
(Court of the Moon and Stars)
(Continued)

INITIAL PLANTING OF FLOWERS AND BULBS

Blue Perfection Violas.
Jersey Gem Violas.
Jacob de Witt Dutch Iris.
D. Haring Dutch Iris.
Bismarck Hyacinths.
Baronne de la Tonnaye Tulip.

Heliotrope Tulip.
Lilac Wonder Tulip.
Calceolaria Golden Giant.
Calceolaria tomentosa. Peru.
Red Ranunculus.

EAST LONG COURT
(Court of Reflections)

HORTICULTURAL COLOR SCHEME: RED

TREES AND SHRUBS

Eucalyptus ficifolia. Australia. Two very large specimens beneath the Arch of the Winds.

Ligustrum japonicum. Japanese Privet. Very tall trees on the side terraces and bordering the two pools.

Prunus pissardii. Asia. At base of walls.

Crataegus. Europe. Specimens on either side of the base of the arch.

Populus nigra italica. Europe and southwestern Asia. Specimens on either side of the base of the arch.

Rhododendron cornubia.

Berberis atropurpurea.

Abelia grandiflora. A garden hybrid (*A. chinensis* and *A. uniflora*), both parents natives of China.

Nandina domestica. China and Japan.

Cydonia japonica. Japan.

Red Geraniums.

Cotoneaster pannosa. Southwest China.

Baby Red Fuchsias. The Fuchsias are mostly natives of tropical America (three or four are from New Zealand).

The eight items just named, beginning with *Rhododendron cornubia,* have been used as borders along the balustrade of the terraces and at the base of the walls, also flanking steps.

INITIAL PLANTING OF FLOWERS AND BULBS

"Tango" Red Pansies.
Bronze Pansies.
Cardinal Pansies.
Lobelia cardinalis in the two pools.
Pride of Haarlem Tulips.
Indian Chief Tulips.

Red Ranunculus.
Red Water Lilies in the two pools.
Red Passion Vines.
Bougainvillaea lateritia. Belongs to the Four-o'Clock Family (Nyctaginaceae). On the walls of the terraces.

EAST SQUARE COURT
(Court of Flowers)

Horticultural Color Scheme: All Colors

TREES AND SHRUBS

Eucalyptus viminalis. Australia. In the corners of the sunken-fountain area.

Eucalyptus cornuta. Australia. Flanking loggia entrances.

Eucalyptus polyanthemos. Australia. In corners.

Crataegus. Europe. At the base of the Arch of the Winds and at the entrance from the Temples of the East.

Populus nigra italica. Europe and Asia. At entrance from the Temples of the East.

Cistus, pink.

Grevillea florida. Australasia.

Erica melanthera. African Heath. Africa.

Fuchsia, Cascade.

Nandina domestica. China and Japan.

Eugenia myrtifolia. Australian Brush Cherry. A member of the Myrtle Family. Australia.

Cistus, white.

Rhododendron, Pink Pearl.

Fuchsias in variety.

Choisya ternata. Mexico.

Lonicera nitida. Western China.

The eleven items just named, beginning with Cistus, are used as borders at base of walls and terraces.

Fatsia japonica (or, *Aralia sieboldii*). Japan. In the fountain.

Strelitzia reginae. Bird-of-Paradise Flower. South Africa. In the fountain.

Gunnera manicata. Brazil. In the fountain.

Alsophila and *Dicksonia.* Around the corner fountains.

Datura arborea. Peruvian Andes. Around the corner fountains.

INITIAL PLANTING OF FLOWERS AND BULBS

Bronze Pansies.

Orange King Tulips.

Swanenburgh White Tulips.

John McLaren Tulips.

Red-flowering Peaches in tubs.

THE TOWER OF THE SUN FROM THE COURT OF THE
MOON AND STARS—NIGHT ILLUMINATION

SOUTH GARDEN
(Enchanted Garden)

Horticultural Color Scheme: Pink Predominating, and Some Blue

TREES AND SHRUBS

Quercus agrifolia. Coast Live Oak. California and Lower California. Thirty trees, from twenty to thirty feet high, obtained for the most part from the Stanford Campus. Used in corners.

Taxus baccata. English Yew. Europe. Five very large specimens flanking pylons.

Taxus baccata var. *elegantissima.* Europe. Five large specimens flanking pylons.

Acacia melanoxylon, standards. Australia. One hundred used in these gardens.

Cedrus deodara. Deodar Cedar. The Himalayas. Four large specimens used.

Pinus radiata. Monterey Pine. California. Twenty specimens used.

Pittosporum eugenioides. New Zealand.

Escallonia organensis, and *E. rosea.* Used at the perimeter of gardens and bordering the English yews. *Escallonia organensis* is a native of Brazil; *E. rubra* and *E. rosea,* of Chile.

Ligustrum ovalifolium. California Privet. Japan. More than one hundred ten-inch specimens used.

Rhododendron Pink Pearl.

Rhododendron roseum elegans.

Rhododendron Alice.

Raphiolepis japonica. Japan.

Buxus suffruticosa. Europe, Asia.

Diosma. South Africa. Probably *Diosma ericoides,* the one commonly grown in the open in California.

INITIAL PLANTING OF FLOWERS AND BULBS

Brigadier Tulips.
Clara Butt Tulips.
Farncombe Sanders Tulips.
Frans Hals Tulips.
Inglescombe Yellow Tulips.
Prince of Orange Tulips.
Princess Elizabeth Tulips.
Scarlet Admiral Tulips.
White Marguerites.
White Larkspur.

Almond Stock.
Jersey Gem Violas.
Blue Perfection Violas.
Snow-white Pansies.
Giant Sea-blue Pansies.
Cardinal Pansies.
Prince Henry Pansies.
Emperor William Pansies.
Innocence Hyacinths.
Mignonette.

PLANTS

Leonotis leonurus. South Africa.
Cupressus macrocarpa. California.
Eucalyptus globulus. Australia.
Eucalyptus globulus var. *compacta*. Australia.
Ericas in variety.
Apricot Violas.
Calendula.
Marigolds.
Acacia melanoxylon. Australia.

Laurocerasus officinalis. Southeastern Europe to Persia.
Pinus radiata. California.
Cedrus deodara. The Himalayas.
Ligustrum japonicum. Japan.
Cedrus atlantica. Morocco.
Taxus baccata. Europe.
Quercus agrifolia. California and Lower California.

AVENUE TREES

Platanus orientalis. Asia Minor (also southeastern Europe to India).
Olea europaea. Mediterranean region.
Acacia verticillata. Australia.
Acacia dealbata. Australia.

Acacia baileyana. Australia.
Acacia mollissima. Australia.
Acacia melanoxylon. Australia.
Salix.

Grau photo

ONE OF THE SOUTH TOWERS AT NIGHT

177

LATIN-AMERICAN GROUP

Outside main entrance: *Laurus nobilis*, the Classical Laurel; *Cotoneaster francheti*, of western China; *Euonymus japonicus*, of Japan.

Inside main entrance: *Euonymus japonicus aureovariegatus*, and *Euonymus japonicus*, of Japan; Toyon (*Photinia arbutifolia*), of California, also well known as Christmas Berry; Bronze Wallflower.

North side of Guatemalan pavilion: Olearia.

South side of Guatemalan pavilion: *Arbutus unedo*, the Strawberry Tree of Spain, first cousin of the Californian Madroño; *Cestrum elegans*, of Mexico; Toyon (*Photinia arbutifolia*), of California; Bronze Wallflower.

Inside small patio: Paul's Scarlet Rose; Abutilon Orange; Oriental Poppy (*Papaver somniferum*); Red Salvia.

North side of Costa Rican, Panamanian, and El Salvadorian pavilions: *Araucaria imbricata*, the Monkey-puzzle Tree of Chile; Aloe; *Coronilla glauca*, of southern Europe; Agave.

South side of Costa Rican, Panamanian, and El Salvadorian pavilions: Hibiscus, fifty specimens; Sparmannia; *Bougainvillaea braziliensis*, of Brazil; *Dombeya wallichii*, probably of Madagascar; Banana; *Billbergia nutans*, of Brazil.

Mexican pavilion: Banana; Tritoma, of South Africa; mixed Tulips; Double Red-flowering Peaches; *Punica granatum*, of southern Asia and the Near East; Castor Beans; *Cytisus racemosus*, of Teneriffe Island; Vitis (Evergreen).

Ecuadorian pavilion: *Nandina domestica*, of Japan and China; Blue Columbine.

Chilean pavilion: *Euonymus japonicus*, of Japan; Banksia Rose; Loquat.

Under olive tree in court: Hibiscus; Baby Red Fuchsia.

Under *Photinia serrulata* in court: Hydrangea; *Myrtus communis*, of southern Europe and the Near East.

Around bandstand in court: *Clematis jackmanii*, a hybrid; *Pleroma grandiflora*; Cascade Fuchsia; mixed Fuchsias; *Myrtus communis*, of southern Europe and the Near East.

Along lagoon: *Ligustrum aureum; Acacia latifolia*, of Australia; Red and Yellow Lantana.

Outside the entrance to the Court of Spain: *Araucaria imbricata;* Blue Agave.

Inside the entrance: Loquat; Elm; Poplar; Paul's Scarlet Rose.

Along the walls of the Court of Spain: *Fremontia mexicana*, of southern California; *Magnolia soulangeana;* Pink Passiflora; Red Passiflora; mixed Tulips; Cardinal Pansy.

PACIFIC AREA

Acacia melanoxylon, standards. Australia.
Photinia serrulata. China and Japan.
Myoporum laetum. New Zealand.
Eucalyptus polyanthemos. Australia.
Eucalyptus globulus. Australia.
Ficus macrophylla. Australia.
Eugenia myrtifolia. East India.
Eucalyptus cornuta. Australia.
Betula alba. Northern regions of Asia, Europe, and North America.
Eucalyptus ficifolia. Australia.
Prunus persica. Asia.
Laurocerasus officinalis. Southeastern Europe to Persia.
Eucalyptus globulus var. *compacta.* Australia.
Eucalyptus cinerea. Australia.
Italian Oak. Southern Europe.
Taxus baccata. Europe, North Africa, and western Asia.

Platanus orientalis. Southeastern Europe to India.
Olea europaea. Mediterranean region.
Salix babylonica. China.
Photinia arbutifolia. California.
Coprosma baueri. New Zealand.
Acacia latifolia. Australia.
Acacia floribunda. Australia.
Ceanothus thyrsiflorus.
Euonymus japonicus. China and Japan.
Maytenus boarii. Chile.
Acacia verticillata. Australia.
Umbellularia californica.
Araucaria excelsa. Chile.
Cryptomeria japonica. China and Japan.
Ilex aquifolium. Southern Europe to China.
Chamaerops humilis. Western Mediterranean region.
Trachycarpus excelsa. Japan.

WESTERN FRONTAGES

Trachycarpus excelsa. Japan.
Washingtonia filifera and *W. robusta.* Southern California.
Phoenix canariensis. Canary Islands.
Leptospermum laevigatum. Australia.
Arundo donax. Mediterranean region and southern Asia.
Chamaerops humilis. Western Mediterranean.
Dracaena indivisa. New Zealand.

Mesembryanthemum. Twenty-one shades.
Cortaderia argentea. Pampas Grass. Chile.
Phormium tenax. New Zealand Flax.
Bamboo.
Escallonia. Many (fifty or more) species, all from South America.
Tritomas in variety. South Africa.
Eucalyptus, few.

Grau photo

ELEPHANT TOWERS AT NIGHT

Moulin photo

FOUNTAIN, ENCHANTED GARDEN, NIGHT

PLANTING MATERIAL USED IN THE CALIFORNIA-BUILDING GROUP

Abelia grandiflora.
Abies grandis (Fir).
Agapanthus umbellatus.
Agave americana.
Ageratum.
Araucaria bidwilli.
Arbutus unedo.
Azalea indica.
Azara microphylla.
Begonia semperflorens.
Beloperone guttata.
Bougainvillaea (giant specimens).
Buxus japonica.
Calendula.
Camellia (assorted varieties).
Canna (assorted varieties).
Carrissa grandiflora.
Ceanothus arboreus.
Ceanothus cyaneus.
Ceanothus thyrsiflorus.
Chamaecyparis lawsoniana.
Chamaecyparis lawsoniana alumi.
Chamaecyparis lycopodiodes.
Chamaerops excelsa (Palm).
Chamaerops humilis (Palm).
Chorizema illicifolium.
Chrysanthemum.
Cineraria (hybrids).
Cocculus laurifolius.
Cocos arechaveletana (Palm).
Cocos australis (Palm).
Cocos plumosa (Palm).
Coniata racemosus.
Cordiateria argentium.
Cotoneaster microphylla.
Cryptomeria japonica.
Cryptomeria japonica elegans.
Cupressus knightiana.
Cycas revoluta (Sago "Palm").
Cyclamen.
Dahlia (assorted colors).

Delphinium.
Deodar.
Diosma reevsii.
Espaliered fruit trees.
Eugenia hookeriana.
Eugenia myrtifolia.
Euonymus japonica.
Fatsia japonica.
Ferns (assorted varieties).
Ficus macrophylla.
Fremontia mexicana.
Fuchsia Black Prince.
Genista racemosa.
Geranium Kovaleski (red).
Geraniums, Ivy, white.
Geraniums, salmon pink.
Geraniums, single white.
Giant Bamboo.
Hedera helix (English Ivy).
Hibiscus (assorted).
Hollyhocks (assorted colors).
Hypericum moserianum.
Iris (assorted varieties).
Iris Alcazar.
Iris Herriott.
Iris magnifica.
Italian Cypress.
Ivy (variegated and green).
Jasminum grandiflorum.
Jasminum lucidum.
Jasminum primulinum.
Jasminum stephanense.
Juniperus chinensis.
Juniperus virginiana (Red Cedar).
Kentia forsteriana (Palm).
Kumquats.
Lantana.
Laurocerasus officinalis (Cherry Laurel).
Laurus nobilis (Laurel).
Leptospermum laevigatum (Hedge).
Libocedrus decurrens (Incense Cedar).

183

Ligustrum japonicum (Privet).
Lobelia.
Lonicera hildebrandii (Honeysuckle).
Magnolia grandiflora.
Mahonia illicifolia.
Marguerites, yellow.
Mesembryanthemum speciosum.
Myrtus microphylla compacta.
Nerium bush, creamy white.
Nerium bush, salmon pink.
Olea europaea (Olive Trees).
Oleanders (rich white).
Orange Trees (Valencia).
Pansies, giant.
Petunias.
Persea americana (Avocado).
Phoenix reclinata (Palm).
Phormium tenax (New Zealand Flax).
Picea excelsa (Norway Spruce).
Pinus attenuata (Knob Cone Pine).
Pinus canariensis.
Pinus densiflora.
Pinus, dwarf.
Pinus radiata (Monterey Pine).
Pinus strobus (Eastern White Pine).
Pittosporum crassifolia.
Pittosporum tobira.

Pittosporum undulatum.
Pleroma splendens.
Quercus agrifolia (Oak).
Ranunculus (Buttercup).
Rhamnus alaternus.
Rhododendron californica.
Rhododendron hybrids.
Ribes speciosum (nondeciduous).
Roses (standard type) (assorted varieties).
Rosebushes.
Schinus molle (California Pepper Trees).
Snapdragons.
Spartium junceum.
Strelitzia regina (Bird-of-Paradise plant).
Taxus baccata (Yew).
Thuja plicata (Arbor Vitae).
Tuberous Begonias.
Ulmus parvifolia (Evergreen Elm).
Umbellularia californica (California
    Laurel).
Violas.
Violas, "Radio."
Virburnum tinus.
Washingtonia filifera (Palm).
Wisteria.
Yucca whipplei (Quixote Plant).

184

Roberts & Roberts photo

PACIFICA—NIGHT ILLUMINATION

185

GROUND PLAN OF THE EXPOSITION
WITH GUIDE TO COURTS AND BUILDINGS

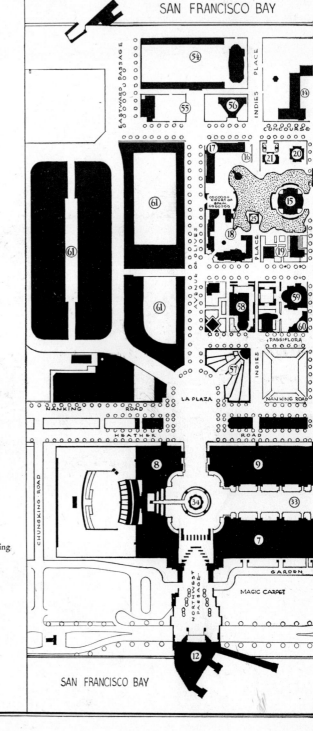

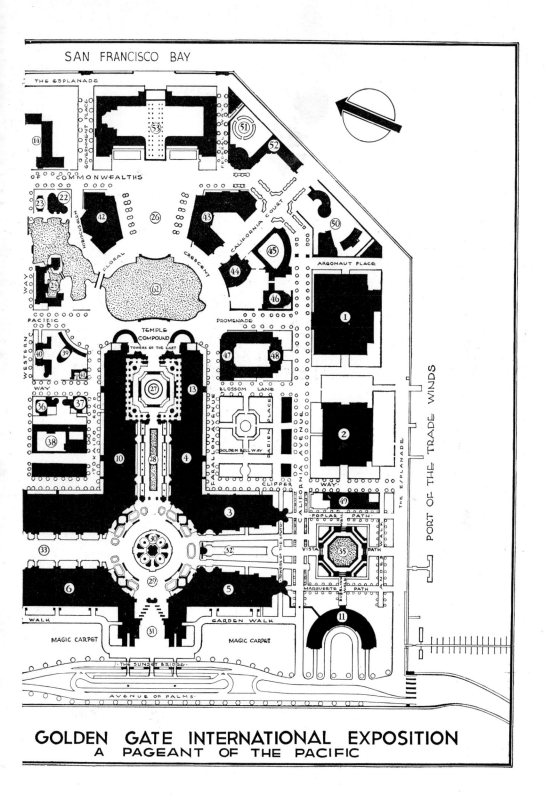

GOLDEN GATE INTERNATIONAL EXPOSITION
A PAGEANT OF THE PACIFIC